D1575577

Tennessee's
Indian
Peoples

Tennessee's Indian Peoples

From White Contact

to Removal, 1540–1840

BY RONALD N. SATZ

PUBLISHED IN COOPERATION WITH

The Tennessee Historical Commission

THE UNIVERSITY OF TENNESSEE PRESS

KNOXVILLE

⚜ TENNESSEE THREE STAR BOOKS / *Paul H. Bergeron, General Editor*

This series of general-interest books about significant Tennessee topics is sponsored jointly by the Tennessee Historical Commission and the University of Tennessee Press. Inquiries about manuscripts should be addressed to Professor Bergeron, History Department, University of Tennessee.

Library of Congress Cataloging in Publication Data

Satz, Ronald N.
  Tennessee's Indian peoples.

  (Tennessee three star books)
  Bibliography: p.
  Includes index.
  1. Indians of North America—Tennessee. I. Title.
II. Series.
E78.T3S24   970.'004'97   77-21634
ISBN 0-87049-231-4

6-4-84

Cover photograph: Sequoyah's Cherokee syllabary, courtesy of The Thomas Gilcrease Institute of American History and Art.

RONALD N. SATZ is Dean of Graduate Studies and Research and teaches history at the University of Tennessee at Martin. In addition to numerous articles and book reviews, his published work includes *American Indian Policy in the Jacksonian Era* (1975). He has received fellowships from both the Ford Foundation and the National Endowment for the Humanities. Professor Satz is currently a member of the Editorial Advisory Board of the *American Indian Quarterly*.

For my wife and children:

Christa and Ani and Jakob

Contents

ILLUSTRATIONS

Tennessee's
Indian
Peoples

1. Introduction

Like American Indians everywhere, the Indians who once made their homes in the hills, valleys, and plains of Tennessee have usually been pictured in history books as little more than natural phenomena, creatures of the pristine wilderness who unfortunately but inevitably fell victim to the progress of the white man. Tennessee was theirs at the beginning of history, when wolves still roamed the forests and rivers ran clear and pure. They were children of nature, untamed and unspoiled, moving through the forests as noiselessly as the wind, subsisting on wild game and berries, and occasionally exhibiting that fierce cruelty that is to be expected from forest dwellers, as when a cougar slaughters a helpless deer. Seen in this way, the Indians are but a part of the natural history of Tennessee. They merely set the stage for the unfolding of the human drama that began with the coming of the first Spanish explorers.

But in truth their story is not so simple. The Indians of Tennessee were not innocent children of nature, fundamentally different from Europeans. They were men and women—human beings. Theirs is not a nature story. It is a human story that reaches back over 11,000 years.

Probably the first people to roam the great valley of the Tennessee River were small bands of nomadic Ice Age hunters. These were the Paleo-Indians, descendants of Asian people who came to North America across a land bridge that connected Alaska and Siberia. Today North America and Siberia are separated by 56 miles of fogbound, choppy water; but during at least two separate periods between 50,000 and 10,000 years ago the vast amounts of water locked up in the glaciers of the Ice Age lowered the level of the Bering Sea and created between the two continents a land bridge which at times was several hundred miles wide. In a series of migrations, Asian hunters moved across to North America following herds of the large game animals of the era—mammoths and straight-horned bison, among others. The diversity of languages spoken by North American Indians of later times is partly accounted for by these different waves of migrations, as well as by the linguistic changes that naturally occur over time when groups become geographically and culturally separate from each other. The common Asian origin of American Indians shows most clearly in such shared physical characteristics as a brownish skin tone, prominent cheekbones, dark eyes, sparse body hair, and coarse, straight, black hair.

The Paleo-Indians of 11,000 years ago had a way of life similar to that of the Upper Paleolithic people of Asia and Europe. They did not live in permanent settlements but moved from camp to camp. The locations of these temporary camps were determined by the movements of game herds and the seasonal availability of wild plant food. Although the Paleo-Indians left behind in these camps little by which their presence could later be discerned, there is evidence that these nomadic hunters camped and hunted in virtually every part of Tennessee.

Over a long period of time, as the Paleo-Indians and their descendants spread far and wide to occupy most of North and South America, the Ice Age gradually came to an end. The earth warmed; the environment changed. In some parts of North America forests grew where none had been before. Deer, elk, and moose thrived, whereas the huge, cold-adapted animals gradually disappeared. Beginning around 8,000 B.C. a new Indian lifeway began taking shape. This was the Archaic tradition.

Instead of ranging limitlessly in pursuit of large game, the Archaic Indians began to exploit intensively more well-defined territories. Compared to their Paleo ancestors, they lived a more settled life. Their population increased and, indicative of their technological advancement, they began making a greater variety of stone objects, some of which were beautifully polished and of undeniable artistic worth. But the Archaic Indians of Tennessee did not live in permanent villages. These people moved with the seasons, gathering within their territories the varied resources of the forests—nuts, roots, seeds, and berries, as well as fowl, small game, and larger browsing animals. Large game was hunted with short spears ejected from spear-throwers that served as an extension of a man's arm and greatly increased the force of the missiles. Domesticated dogs may also have been used in hunting. In addition the Archaic Indians depended upon the rivers for subsistence. They fished the streams and they collected mollusks, too, as indicated by the shell mounds found today along the Tennessee and Cumberland rivers.

Gradually, over thousands of years, the cultural patterns of the Archaic

---

(*Above*): Use of the spear thrower. Courtesy of *South Carolina Wildlife*. (*Below*): polished stones used by Archaic hunters as spear-thrower weights. Courtesy of Frank H. McClung Museum, University of Tennessee, Knoxville.

Indians changed. Their material life became more complex, and so presumably did their societies. By 1,000 B.C. they were so different from the early Archaic people that a new cultural tradition—the Woodland—can be said to have begun. One of the hallmarks of this new lifeway was the introduction of pottery. By the Middle Woodland period, the Indians of Tennessee were living in small villages. Food-gathering groups probably continued to move out to temporary camps at different times of the year, but the base villages seem to have been permanent. Woodland houses were oval or circular structures made by placing the ends of small saplings in the ground and bending them over to form a dome-shaped framework, usually covered with sheets of bark.

The Woodland Indians were innovators. Over the years they developed pottery to take the place of vessels carved out of soapstone and, by the latter half of the Woodland period, the bow and arrow to replace the spear. Another Woodland innovation was the emergence of the rudiments of agriculture to supplement the hunting and gathering pattern of the Archaic lifeway. Woodland times may be viewed as a period of transition leading to a way of life in which agriculture played a larger role than it did for the Archaic hunter-gatherers. There is evidence to indicate that squash, gourds, and sunflowers were the first plants grown by the Tennessee Indians, these domesticates first appearing late in the Archaic period. The Woodland people continued to grow these crops and also may have developed crops of their own. For thousands of years their ancestors had gathered the seeds of wild weeds—sumpweed, chenopodium, and maygrass. The Woodland Indians continued this practice and perhaps even began to cultivate some of these plants. At some time during the Woodland period, these people began cultivation of a new crop, corn, that had been introduced from the south.

The Woodland people were the first Indians of Tennessee to build mounds, many of which may still be seen in the state—some of them created by Woodland Indians, others by their descendants of a later tradition. Those built by Woodland Indians are burial mounds: dome-shaped earthen tombs for the dead. But not all people of the Woodland tradition were buried in mounds. Scholars are not certain of why some individuals were given these elaborate burials and others were not, but it is obvious that a complex social and religious structure was in operation, affecting to some degree the lives of most Woodland Indians.

This Indian burial mound is located on the agricultural campus of the University of Tennessee, Knoxville. Courtesy of University of Tennessee Photographic Services, Knoxville.

Around A.D. 900 a new social development arose among the natives living along the Mississippi River between present-day St. Louis, Missouri, and Vicksburg, Mississippi. The cultivation of corn and beans made agriculture more productive than ever before. Greater populations could now be supported. Villages and towns expanded. Political structures became more centralized, religion more formalized. Social organization became more stratified. Mounds were built on a larger scale than ever before and their function changed. No longer simply burial mounds, the new earthen mounds were shaped like flat-topped pyramids and served as platforms for temples, council chambers, and chiefs' houses.

This new tradition—the Mississippian—had a profound influence in the South. It spread throughout the region, partly by the movement of ideas and partly by the actual movement of people who migrated from the Mississippi Valley to settle intrusively among the Woodland Indians elsewhere.

In time all the natives of Tennessee took on at least some of the trappings of the Mississippian cultural tradition. In the western part of the state, platform mound sites are found along the Mississippi River and its tributary streams, including the Forked Deer and Obion rivers. There are numerous sites in the Cumberland River Valley in Middle Tennessee. But the southern half of the central basin area apparently did not have as dense a population during the Mississippian period. In East Tennessee, sites with Mississippian traits are found from Chattanooga northeastward into the remote valleys of the headwaters of the Tennessee River. Although the Mississippian Indians were living in some parts of Tennessee when the first Europeans arrived, archaeologists are unable to trace a direct connection between these people and the more familiar names found in recorded history—such as the Cherokees, Chickasaws, Creeks, and Shawnees. Even so, the Cherokees and Creeks in particular were certainly influenced by the Mississippian culture and, according to one school of thought, some of them had Mississippian ancestors.

The Mississippian Indians were a settled people, some living in large towns, whereas others occupied small rural hamlets. They were farmers and hunters, tilling the fertile river valleys and searching out game in the forests. They gathered together in the public buildings of their towns for religious observances and political meetings. They entertained themselves at home and

---

(*Above*): This 1597 map may be the earliest showing Cherokee Indian towns. From Bureau of American Ethnology *Fifth Annual Report*, courtesy of Special Collections, University of Tennessee Library, Knoxville. (*Below*): De Soto's crossbowmen fire upon Indian warriors. From Pierre Richelet, *Histoire della Conquesta de la Florida*.

in public with stories, games, and dances. Like men everywhere, they fought wars, and they sought peace. And always they endeavored to live according to the principles of their beliefs. Their chiefs were men of considerable power. Some of them lived in special houses on the tops of mounds and were carried about on litters when they went aboard among their people. But not even the most powerful of these chiefs possessed the treasures of silver and gold that the Spanish conquistador Hernando de Soto was seeking when he invaded their territories.

De Soto and his 600 soldiers and followers were the first Europeans to set foot on Tennessee soil. Late in the spring of 1540, after having marched in the previous year from Florida through Georgia and South Carolina, the Spanish army is believed to have followed the Hiwassee River into the Great Valley of East Tennessee, where the invaders were received peacefully by the Cherokee Indians. Finding no gold or silver to be plundered, the soldiers rested there, refreshing themselves and their weary horses, and then followed the Tennessee River downstream to the Creek town of Chiaha on an island near present-day Chattanooga. Here they camped for nearly the entire month of June. From Chiaha they sent out an expedition to find the mysterious "Chisca province" in the hilly country of East Tennessee, which the Chiahans claimed contained rich gold and silver deposits. But no treasure was found.

The Spanish conquistador's journey among these peoples was a cruel one. De Soto extorted burden bearers and women from chiefs who had befriended him. He used the Indians harshly, ordering individuals put to death for the slightest cause. As a result, relations between the invaders and the native peoples deteriorated steadily, although open warfare did not erupt until de Soto's party reached the town of Mabila in Alabama. Here the Indians launched a surprise attack that inflicted heavy losses on the Spaniards. Thereafter, de Soto's forces literally had to fight their way through Alabama. In late December they entered the territory of the Chickasaw Indians in northern Mississippi. Here the soldiers spent the winter, enduring continual harassment from Chickasaw raiding parties. In the spring, de Soto's men made a hasty departure and on May 8, 1541, reached the "province of Quizquiz," which bordered the Mississippi River and was inhabited by a people who were hostile to the Chickasaws. The province of Quizquiz may have included Chucalissa, the restored Indian town six miles south of downtown Memphis, but more likely the province was farther south of Memphis. In spite of the hostility of the natives, de Soto stayed more than a month at Quizquiz in order to build barges, which he used to cross the Mississippi River, leaving behind him the region later known as Tennessee.

Information about which particular Indian tribes lived where within the present borders of Tennessee is fragmentary for a period of about 150 years following de Soto's visit. Only after the late 1600s, when Europeans began to have sustained contact with the region's people, can the native residents be identified with certainty. At that time members of the Cherokee and Chickasaw tribes laid claim to East and West Tennessee, respectively, and had overlapping claims in Middle Tennessee. In addition some Shawnees may have had villages in the Cumberland River Valley of Middle Tennessee.

During the early historic period, the Cherokees were the largest Indian tribe in the entire South. According to various estimates, there were between fifty to eighty towns scattered among the southern Appalachian Mountains, with a total population of perhaps 22,000 people. The Cherokee settlements were divided into three regions, each with its own dialect of the Cherokee language. The heart of the Cherokee Nation was the Middle Settlements in present-day western North Carolina. Farther south, in northwestern South Carolina and the neighboring portion of Georgia, were the Lower Towns. Just "over the hills" from these two regions were the Overhill Towns of East Tennessee, the most remote, independent, and dynamic region of the early Cherokees. The Overhill Towns were situated mainly along the lower course of the Little Tennessee River, but there were also some communities on the Tellico and Hiwassee rivers and perhaps on the Little Pigeon River as well. In the fertile valleys of these rivers lay such towns as Chatuga, Chilhowee, Chota, Great Hiwassee, Great Tellico, Setticoe, Tallassee, Tannassee or Tanasi, Tomotley, Toqua, and Tuskegee. First Tanasi, then Great Tellico, and finally Chota served as the capital of the Overhill Towns. The Cherokees claimed as their hunting range a vast territory that extended far beyond their settlements and included all of East and Middle Tennessee.

The Cherokee claim to Middle Tennessee was challenged by several tribes, including the Chickasaws, whose hunting territory encompassed West Tennessee. While the Chickasaws were not a large tribe—numbering only about 4,500—they were strong militarily, with a reputation for ferocity and courage. They did not have permanent villages in Tennessee; their principal towns, fewer than six in number, were located in north-central Mississippi. Nevertheless, the abundant game in West Tennessee made that area a favorite hunting ground for these people. They built hunting camps in the region, clearing away the underbrush and some trees to build temporary shelters near creeks, rivers, or springs. No one knows why the Chickasaws never took up permanent residence in West Tennessee, but an interesting, though dubious, explanation was offered by Memucan Hunt Howard, a nineteenth-century land agent:

> I have heard it said that the Indians, when asked why none of them lived permanently in West Tennessee, replied that it leaked too much. For a time

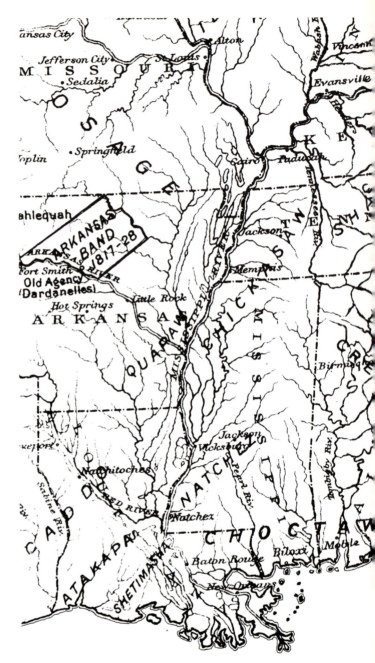

This map by James Mooney shows the location of Tennessee's Indians
their southern neighbors. From Bureau of American Ethnology *Ninetee*

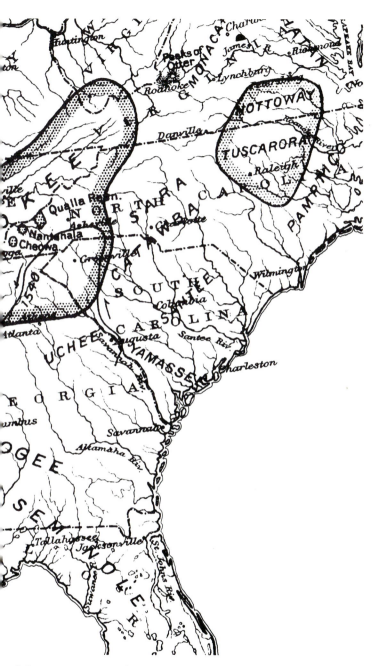

ual Report, courtesy of Special Collections, University of Tennessee rary, Knoxville.

after I first went there I thought it rained, hailed, thundered and lightened with more wind than I had known elsewhere.

Although both the Cherokees and the Chickasaws claimed Middle Tennessee, neither tribe had permanent settlements there. A third group—the Shawnees—were active hunters and traders in the Cumberland River Valley, however, and may have occupied scattered villages in that area. The Shawnees were a people centered originally in the Ohio Valley, but their range extended south through Kentucky to the Cumberland Valley and beyond. Their presence in Middle Tennessee brought them into continual conflict with both the Cherokees and Chickasaws, and the Shawnee people were eventually driven from the area by these two tribes in the early eighteenth century.

To the south of Tennessee—in Georgia, Alabama, and northern Florida— lived the main body of the Creek Indians. The Creeks embodied a large and powerful confederacy of numerous small tribes who spoke different but mostly related languages. A few Creek towns at one time were located as far north as the Chattanooga area and perhaps even farther up the Tennessee River. But in the early 1700s the Cherokees pushed them out of Tennessee.

Remnant bands of at least two other tribes had homes within the boundaries of Tennessee. In the early eighteenth century the Natchez Indians of the lower Mississippi Valley were driven from their homeland in a disastrous war with the French. The refugees scattered, finding homes with different tribes throughout the South. Some of the Natchez Indians settled among the Overhill Cherokees of Tennessee, as did some of the Yuchi Indians. At one time the Yuchis lived in South Carolina and Georgia near the Savannah River, but in the eighteenth century the British pushed them from that area. Most of the Yuchi exiles went to live among the Creeks, yet in the early nineteenth century a number of them were also known to be living among the Cherokees near present-day Cleveland, Tennessee. Yuchis may have lived in Tennessee even before this, but the record of their early history is confused and uncertain. According to one account, a group of Yuchis once lived in Tennessee near the mouth of the Hiwassee River and were nearly exterminated in a desperate battle with the Cherokees at the Uchee Old Fields in present-day Meigs County.

It can be seen, then, that no single Indian tribe lived predominantly within the boundaries of Tennessee. The Overhill Cherokees, however, not only had the largest and strongest contingent in the region but also had their permanent homes in the state. They remained in their Tennessee homeland until forced away by white Americans in the nineteenth century.

Of all the different tribes who lived in Tennessee, only the Chickasaws and Creeks spoke related languages, and even these two languages were only as closely related as German is to English—they were in the same language family, Muskogean, but were not mutually intelligible. The Natchez spoke a language remotely related to Muskogean but so different from the language of any other tribe as to be called a language isolate. The languages spoken by all other tribes in Tennessee differed from each other and from Muskogean as much as English differs from Arabic. The Cherokees, for instance, spoke an Iroquoian language that was related to the languages spoken by the Iroquois confederacy in the Northeast, but the Shawnees spoke an Algonkian language, related to that of the Delawares and tribes found along the Atlantic seaboard. In fact, it is astounding to contemplate the great diversity of languages once spoken by these early Tennessee peoples. And yet, even though they spoke languages so foreign to one another, the Indians who lived and hunted in the hills, valleys, and plains of the region were more alike in their manner of living than they were different.

2. Native Culture and Society

James Adair, an eighteenth-century colonial trader who lived for over thirty years among the southern Indians, commented that although the various tribes differed from one another in particular rites and customs, they all agreed remarkably "in essentials." In Tennessee only the Shawnees, whose cultural ties were more with the Northeast than the South, differed from the other native peoples to any appreciable extent, and even these differences were of minor importance in the face of overriding similarities. It is possible, therefore, in spite of particular variances among the tribes, to obtain a general view of Indian life in Tennessee.

The historic Indians of Tennessee continued the practice of their ancestors in locating their towns and hamlets on high banks or hills along the margins of rivers and large streams. Such locations provided easy access to the rich bottom lands that bordered the water courses, while at the same time offering protection from floods and providing a military advantage in case of an enemy attack.

No other soil was so well suited to Indian agriculture as was the alluvial soil of these bottom lands. This sandy loam was loose enough to be worked with Indian hoes, and it possessed the drainage properties favored by corn, the most important native crop. Corn is a hungry plant, quickly depleting the nutrients of a soil, but in bottom lands flooded by standing backwater at least every few years, corn could be grown almost continuously.

The Indians planted their corn in "hills" spaced about three feet apart, allowing three or four stalks to grow in each hill, and sowed beans—the pole variety—in the same hills with the corn so that the bean vines could wind up the stalks. Between the hills of corn and beans, and in separate fields as well, the natives planted gourds, squash, pumpkins, and sunflowers. Contrary to popular notion, these people did not fertilize their crops with dead fish, relying instead on the occasional floodwaters to keep their soil productive.

Agriculture was primarily the work of Indian women, and so too was the gathering of wild vegetable foods. The natives depended heavily on wild roots and tubers (particularly Jerusalem artichokes and greenbriar), nuts (especially chestnuts and hickory nuts), and fruits and berries (chiefly persimmons, plums, and blackberries). The settled Indians of Tennessee also began growing peach and apple trees at a very early time in the colonial period.

Just as the Indian women were responsible for harvesting vegetable foods, it was the men's duty to supply their families with meat. Deer was the primary game animal, although bear, turkey, small game, and waterfowl were also hunted. The men fished the rivers and streams using traps and nets, trotlines, or simply spears and bows and arrows.

The Indians preserved fish, meat, fruit, and vegetables primarily by drying. Some corn, beans, and squash were picked and eaten when young and tender, but most of a season's crop was allowed to grow to maturity and then was harvested and stored in both family and public storehouses. Much of the corn was later soaked in wood-ash lye water to make hominy, which was then cracked or ground into meal for making mush or bread. Nuts were gathered in large quantities from the forests and stored unshelled.

In Mississippian times, before the coming of the Europeans, cooking was done in pottery vessels made by the women. In the eighteenth century, pottery continued to be used, but iron and brass kettles had become popular household items for cooking. Food was eaten from pottery bowls, wooden bowls and plates, and gourd vessels.

When a hunter killed an animal for meat, very little of the slaughter went to waste. Most often the hunters themselves skinned their kills, dressing the hides in a preliminary fashion, but the transformation of the raw, stiff hides into soft, supple clothing depended upon the artistry of the women. Deerskin was the material most widely used for Indian garments, but other skins as well as furs, feathers, and fibers were also utilized. The Indian women, using pieces of animal or bird bone for needles and awls, sewed skins together with sinew and other materials with animal or vegetable fiber. They wore knee-length deerskin skirts that were wrapped about their waists and held in place by either a leather or a woven belt. For warmth females covered their shoulders with mantels of deerskin in mild weather and of muskrat or some other warm fur in winter. The men dressed in breechcloths and sleeveless shirts which hung down to their knees. Both garments were commonly made of deerskin. During hunting trips or in cold weather, the males added leather leggings to their outfits. Both sexes wore leather moccasins with tops that reached halfway up their legs. The men's clothing was generally more highly decorated than the women's, especially after the introduction of European cloth and other trade goods. On ceremonial occasions the apparel varied all the way from the simplest, near nudity, to elaborate and colorful regalia. According to a London newspaper in 1730, several young Cherokee leaders visiting England appeared before the royal family in the following attire:

The Indian King had on a scarlet jacket, but all the rest were naked except an apron [breechcloth] about their middle and a horse's tail hung down behind. Their faces, shoulders, etc., were painted and spotted with red, blue and green. They had bows in their hands and painted feathers in their heads.

The Cherokees created some highly decorative clothes and accessories. Skirts for women and cloaks for both sexes were sometimes made of large feathers taken from wild turkeys and sewn between strips of mulberry fiber. The feathers of more brightly colored birds graced these garments as trimmings, while feathers from eagles and white cranes provided material for headdresses. Frequently the Cherokees decorated their bodies with paint and tattoos, and they often wore bracelets, neckpieces of shell, and earrings. Sometimes they slit their ears and stretched them to an enormous size in order to adorn them with pendants and rings. A Cherokee woman tied her long, black hair with ribbons of various colors, while a man plucked out all of the hair from his head except for the small patch of scalp lock. Frequently dress and ornamentation meant more than warmth or appearance; the two could symbolize the Indian's role and status in society.

Each tribe of the native peoples of Tennessee was divided into clans composed of individuals who believed that all of them were descended from a common ancestor. A clan took its name from an element of nature, often an animal. The Cherokees, for instance, had seven clans, including the Deer, Wolf, Bird, and Paint clans. Members of an Indian clan regarded each other as relatives with a claim upon each other's loyalty and hospitality, even though they might be complete strangers from widely separated towns. Clan relationships cut across town and family life, binding all members in ties that regulated many details of their social relationships. A person could not marry or have sexual relations with another member of the same clan. Except among the Shawnees, children belonged to the clan of their mother. A child's closest adult male relative in this matrilineal system was not his father, who belonged to a different clan, but his mother's brother. Yet even though a father was not considered a blood relative of his children, his relationship with them was nonetheless close and special. Usually, as among the Cherokees, a person could not marry into his father's clan. The Shawnees were exceptional among Tennessee's Indian peoples in that they followed a patrilineal line rather than a

---

The Cherokee men trapped fish in handmade traps (*above*), and the women wove baskets (*below*). Scenes from Oconaluftee Indian Village, courtesy of Cherokee Historical Association.

matrilineal one. For them the kinship system was reversed, with children belonging to the clan of their father.

Female kin typically managed marriage arrangements among the Indians, but men had a voice in choosing their wives; and marriages were not forced. A man could have more than one wife so long as the first wife gave her permission. Co-wives were usually of the same clan, often sisters, and generally got along better than might be expected. Premarital sex was not frowned upon by the Indians so long as both people involved were unmarried and of different clans. After marriage, however, sexual fidelity was valued, though more by some tribes than others. Among the Creeks both men and women were punished for adultery, the clansmen of the offended spouse beating the guilty pair or even disfiguring them by cutting off their ears or noses. The Chickasaws inflicted similar punishment, but only upon the women. The Cherokees, although they did not look favorably upon adultery, did not punish offenders of either sex.

Marriage among the Indians involved a binding relationship between the clans of the husband and the wife. Nowhere was this more apparent than when one of the spouses died. Unless a widowed woman took another husband from her dead husband's clan, she was required to mourn for a long period of time—up to four years among the Creeks and Chickasaws. During the mourning period she was expected to neglect her personal appearance, stay mostly inside her own house, wail regularly each day for her deceased husband, and refrain from intimacy with any man. The dead husband's clan was responsible for making sure she mourned properly, and the women of that clan kept a watch on her. Remarriage into that same clan would end the mourning requirement. But if a widow wanted to remarry into a clan other than that of her late husband, she would have to wait until the long mourning period was over, unless her deceased husband's kinsmen took pity on her and released her from her obligation. A widower was similarly required to mourn the death of his wife, but usually for a much shorter period of time. Among the Cherokees neither men nor women were required to go through a long mourning period.

In Tennessee's Indian societies the two sexes occupied separate though overlapping worlds. Women dominated the domestic scene. Among the Cherokees, Chickasaws, and the Creeks they owned their homes—though their husbands may have built them—and their children belonged to their clans rather than to their husbands' clans. When a woman married she did not move away from her own people, but rather her husband moved in with her. This meant that women seldom found themselves alone among strangers. Although their work was unending, it was usually carried on in familiar company with as much pleasant social interaction taking place as there was hard work accomplished. The prominence of women in Cherokee domestic affairs so startled one male chauvinist European in the early eighteenth century that he wrote, "the women rules the ro[o]st and weres the britches and sometimes will beat thire husbands within an inch of thire life."

It is unlikely that any Indian men were regularly beaten by their wives, but in a matrilineal society a man was always something of an outsider when at home with his wife and her people. In the public arena, however, men were very much in their own world. They served as the politicians, priests, and warriors of their society. European observers often remarked that Indian men were so lazy that they made their women do all the work, while they themselves played games or lounged around their council houses. Although the men did not labor so continuously as women, their work, when it came, was often more strenuous than that of their wives. The men, for instance, cleared the fields for the women and built houses and public buildings. Nonetheless, the men's principal occupations remained hunting and warfare, both of which could demand great physical prowess and endurance.

Indian tribes in Tennessee usually excluded women from most political and religious events. The Cherokees, however, were notable for their liberal attitude toward female participation in public affairs. James Adair wrote that women had such "full liberty" in Cherokee society that these Indians lived under a "petticoat-government." Not only were Cherokee women allowed in council houses, but a woman might earn the title *Agehyagusta* ("Beloved Woman") and be permitted to participate in high-level decision making, including determinations concerning war. Beloved women also had authority to decide whether prisoners of war would be tortured or adopted into one of the clans. As the Englishman Henry Timberlake observed in 1762, beloved women could free "a wretch condemned by the council, and already tied to the stake" by merely waving a swan's wing. Cherokee folklore even contains some tradition of female warriors. Even so, for the most part, Cherokee women remained influential rather than powerful in tribal affairs. Like other Indian women, they spent much of their time engaged in unheralded, laborious duties. When the men were hunting, fishing, or at war, the Cherokee women took care of the family dwellings, gathered firewood, cultivated the crops, prepared animal skins for clothing, made pottery and basketry, collected roots, nuts, and berries, and cared for the children.

The instruction of children in native society was based on a precise division of responsibility by sex. Girls learned from their mothers the domestic arts: how to make pottery, basketry, and clothing; how to plant and care for the crops; how to turn hard kernels of corn and the carcass of a deer into a tasty meal. Boys were taught by their fathers or their mothers' brothers the skills of manhood so essential for success in hunting and warfare. The youngsters learned to make such necessary tools as arrow shafts and bows from hickory wood and blow guns from cane. From the time they were old enough to walk and carry a bow, they practiced stealth and marksmanship. Endurance was enhanced by diving into streams on icy mornings and by challenging one another to contests of pain, such as who could bear the most yellow jacket stings. Warriors placed their young sons on panther skins to bring out in them the qualities of strength and cunning, while their wives placed their daughters on fawn or buffalo-calf skins to make them shy and timid. The Indians disciplined their children with ridicule, shame being harder to bear in native society than pain. Girls were disciplined by their mothers, boys by their maternal uncles—in societies other than the Shawnees. A Shawnee boy was disciplined by his father. The harshest punishment meted out to a child was the use of a length of briar or a comb of dried snake's teeth or other sharp points to scratch the child's skin barely enough to draw blood. It was not the slight pain that made scratching a harsh punishment, but the scratches themselves that remained visible for days, subjecting the child to prolonged ridicule.

Tennessee's Indian peoples singled out children early in life for special training to prepare them for civil and religious offices. Youngsters received lessons during periods of fasting and had regular instruction in traditional history, religious beliefs, rituals, and sacred medicinal formulas.

Native medical practices centered around the belief that all illnesses had mystical causes and that certain herbs possessed effective curing powers when administered by a person who knew how to use them to manipulate spiritual forces. A wide spectrum of medical knowledge existed in Indian society: one curer might know only enough to handle minor ailments, whereas another might have knowledge great enough to deal with any illness. Women as well as men could be curers, but men were more likely to be highly trained and thereby possess deeper knowledge and greater spiritual power in their communities.

Most illnesses were believed to be caused by animal spirits intruding themselves into one's body. A curer would attempt to heal a sick person by simultaneously administering the proper herbal medicine and uttering an incantation to a spiritual adversary of the invading spirit. For instance, if the healer believed that the spirit of a deer was causing the illness, he might call in a spiritual dog to chase it away. Native healers believed that offending spirits caused illnesses by mystically intruding a foreign object into the patient's body without leaving a wound. By skillful sleight of hand a curer would climax his healing performance by supposedly extracting the troublesome object, holding it up for all to see. If a healer felt his power was not great enough to effect a cure, he would say so without shame or loss of face, and the patient would seek help elsewhere.

Some of the herbs employed by Indian healers are recognized today as having medicinal value. Moreover, psychiatrists at the National Institute of Mental Health and the Indian Health Service have recently acknowledged that native healing ceremonies are psychologically beneficial to many contemporary tribesmen even though the therapeutic techniques employed are quite unorthodox compared to those of modern medicine.

Tennessee's Indian peoples placed a high value on both spiritual and physical cleanliness and purity. Regular bathing in nearby streams, often in conjunction with a sweat bath, was a religious and civic duty of southern Indians that had to be carried out even in winter. "In the coldest weather, and when the ground is covered with snow," a European trader noted, "men and children turn out of their warm houses . . . reeking with sweat . . . skip [ping] along . . . till they get to the river, when they instantaneously plunge into it. If the water is frozen, they break the ice with a religious impatience." Bathing supposedly purged the body of the impurities of the previous day. But the effect sought was to a great extent spiritual, so that women, old people, and sick people were allowed to substitute a symbolic sprinkling in place of the actual plunge. The Chickasaws punished anyone careless of personal and household cleanliness by subjecting them to the humiliation of being scratched.

Before most important undertakings, including their religious ceremonies, southern Indian men would drink a strong tea—called "black drink" by the Europeans. After swallowing large quantities of the liquid the men would vomit it up in order to purge impurities, both physical and spiritual, from their bodies, thereby making them cleansed individuals more likely to succeed in their endeavors. Black drink in itself did not cause vomiting, however. It is a caffeine drink similar to *maté* of South America, and the Indians often drank the liquid—without vomiting—while lounging about their council houses talking to their friends.

The council house was the center of town life among the Cherokees, who after the early eighteenth century were the only settled Indians of any number in Tennessee. Up until the arrival of the Europeans a Cherokee town had a tightly clustered settlement pattern with the council house in the center, often atop an earthen mound, an open plaza nearby for public events, dwelling houses crowded closely around, and the whole surrounded by a defensive palisade of upright, closely-set timbers. By the second quarter of the eighteenth century, however, palisades were no longer in general use, and without these walls the settlement pattern of Cherokee towns became more diffuse. The council house—as the focal point for governmental affairs, religious ceremonies, and even social events—remained the central meeting place, but the dwellings of individual families were now scattered along the river valleys in the midst of their agricultural fields.

William Bartram, an eighteenth-century traveler, gave an appealing description of his journey through the Cherokee town of Watauga. Although this town was located in the Middle Settlements of western North Carolina, certainly towns like it must have existed also among the Overhill Cherokees of Tennessee:

> Riding through this large town, the road carried me winding about through their little plantations of Corn, Beans, &c. up to the council-house, which was a very large dome or rotunda, situated on the top of an ancient artificial mount, and here my road terminated. All before me and on every side, appeared little plantations of young Corn, Beans, &c. divided from each other by narrow strips or borders of grass, which marked the bounds of each one's property, their habitation standing in the midst.

Cherokee families ordinarily had two kinds of houses, one for warm weather and one for cold. The summer houses of the eighteenth century were sturdy rectangular buildings, usually not over 16 feet wide but sometimes as long as 60 to 70 feet. In contrast, the winter houses of the period were round—small circular buildings with conical roofs.

The walls of the rectangular summer houses were made of upright saplings imbedded closely together in the ground. Smaller branches were woven around the saplings in basket fashion and plastered with a mixture of clay and grass, after which the walls were usually whitewashed, giving the house a neat appearance. The roof was shingled either with bark or with thinly split wood. The doorway was narrow, not more than two feet wide, and was the only opening except for a smokehole in the peak of the roof. A shallow basin in the center of the packed earth floor served as a hearth, and smoke from the fire usually meandered about in the space beneath the roof before finding its way out the smokehole. The longer of these summer houses contained more than one room—one for cooking, one for sleeping, and sometimes even a third for eating and visiting. The inner walls of Cherokee houses were often covered with colorful mats made of dyed strips of cane. The main articles of furniture served as both couches and beds. Found along almost every wall,

Seating in the Cherokee Council House. From Bureau of American Ethnology *Bulletin 133*, courtesy of Special Collections, University of Tennessee Library, Knoxville.

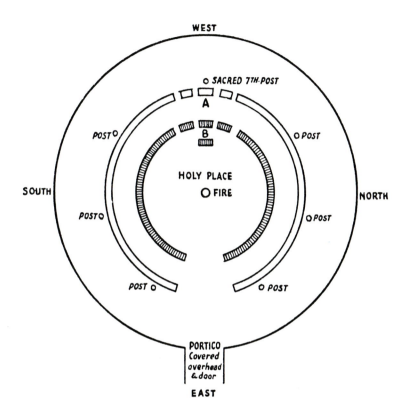

these wooden constructions were cushioned with cane mats and animal skins and supported on posts two to three feet high.

Cherokee winter houses of the eighteenth century were round and entirely covered with a thick layer of earth which served to insulate the small buildings against the cold. Beds similar to those of the summer houses lined the inner walls, and a low fire in the central hearth provided ample warmth. The Europeans called the winter houses "hot houses" and complained of the smoky, stifling heat inside them. Martin Schneider, a Moravian missionary among the Overhill Cherokees in the late eighteenth century, gave this description of the winter house:

> Every Family has besides the Dwelling House still a smaller Hothouse. This has but a very small Opening to creep into it, & this is their Abode in cold Weather; after the Fire which is made in the Middle is burnt down, the coals are covered with Ashes. Their Couches of Cane fixed round about are their Sleeping Places, which they scarce ever leave before 9 o'clock in the Morning. Then they make again Fire for the whole Day & Night they make another. The Old People having but little & the Children, till they are 10 years old, no Cloathes at all, they could not hold it out in cold Weather without such Houses.

The Cherokee council house, or town house, resembled closely the round winter house, but it was much larger. The council house at Chota was so large that it could seat 500 people. A circle of pillars on the inside of a council house supported the roof structure, and seats similar to the beds of the family dwellings were arranged along the walls, except that in the council house these seats were tiered in several rows in amphitheater style. The town fire, or "sacred fire," burned in a central hearth, and the only openings to the building were the small smokehole in the roof and a narrow doorway. The council house was therefore dark and smoky. In the summer, council members often held their meetings in open pavillions.

Unless serious affairs were being conducted in the council house, people who were not busy with other duties often entertained themselves with games. Located near every council house was a chunkey yard, a long, smooth court over which a stone disc about two inches thick and five or six inches in diameter could be swiftly rolled. Most of the time the game of chunkey was

---

(*Above*): Three examples of stone disks used in the chunkey game. From Thomas M. N. Lewis and Madeline Kneberg, *Tribes That Slumber: Indians of the Tennessee Region*. (*Below*): Indian ball game—ball up. Oil on canvas by George Catlin, 1836. Courtesy of National Collection of Fine Arts, Smithsonian Institution.

played by two men, each with a pole eight to ten feet long. One of the players rolled the stone disc with all his might, and as it sped down the court the two contestants raced after it, hurling their poles before them. The winner was the player whose pole landed closest to the spot where the chunkey stone finally rolled to a stop. Although no more than two to four men played at one time, the game usually attracted a crowd of onlookers, most of whom whetted their interest by gambling on the outcome.

Another sport involved many more players—and more gambling as well. It was the ball game, similar to modern lacrosse, in which one town competed against another. The game, played on a long field with goals at each end, could involve as many as one hundred contestants on each team. Ball players were equipped with sticks, which were curved at one end into a small loop that was laced with deerskin thongs to form a pocket for the ball. The ball itself was made of deerskin stuffed with deer hair and sewn together with deer sinew. A point was scored when a team managed to get the ball through the proper goal either by carrying it or hurling it with a ball stick. The team with the ball had to run, fight, and wrestle its way down the field. Players were often injured and occasionally killed, and the Indians called the ball game the "Little Brother of War." To lose was a humiliating defeat for a town, and the losers eagerly sought a rematch.

When the people in a Cherokee town had serious matters to discuss or important decisions to make, they convened in their council house. The town council, which constituted the basic unit of Cherokee local government, was dominated by three groups of elders, referred to as "beloved men," who presided over the "white" tasks of civil life. The first group, which occupied the center of the council house during deliberations, consisted of the town chief and his assistants. The second group was composed of seven elders, one from each of the clans, who formed an advisory council that sat near the town chief. All the rest of the "beloved men" of the community formed the third group of elders who joined the remainder of the town's people in the various clan sections around the sides of the council house. The elders and the younger men in each section probably sat in front of the women and the children. Although the entire population of the community assembled to form the town council, the "beloved men" dominated the proceedings.

The town council served as a forum for reconciling conflicting interests and opinions concerning relations with other Cherokee towns, other Indian tribes, and the European colonies. Also handled by the council were internal matters such as ceremonies and town projects. Because every decision had to be unanimous—the Cherokee ethos stressed harmony and the avoidance of open conflict—discussion of any topic might continue for many days. Although Europeans usually called the town chiefs "kings," these officials actually had no coercive authority. Indeed they had to be patient, restrained, and sensitive to the needs of their people in order to achieve a consensus by compromise or by the withdrawal of groups which could not be accommodated. After the "beloved men" of each clan consulted together to form a single position on each question, they used their influence to win the support of the entire clan. Then each of the seven elders who constituted the advisory council presented the sentiments of his clan to the people assembled in the council house. Debate followed until there was unanimous agreement on the issue. Thus the "white" chief actually administered the day-to-day activities in his community by voluntary consensus through the influence of the "beloved men" of the clans.

War ventures, the often violent ball games, and negotiations with other tribes were known as "red" tasks, and once the town council made a decision involving these activities, the principal warriors were ready to assume their responsibilities as leaders. These "red" leaders were fear-inspiring, experienced warriors who were adept at generating enthusiasm for battle and working within the hierarchical system of the war ranks. In accordance with the Cherokee emphasis on harmony, however, they, like the "white" chiefs, did not have strong coercive powers.

In early historic times, according to recent anthropological studies, the Cherokees had no political authority higher than that of their own town council. Although they shared a national identity as an ethnic group possessing a distinctive character and a common historical and cultural heritage, there was no head of state, no tribal council, and no central authority of any kind. The Cherokee tribe was an aggregate of politically independent towns. The Appalachian Mountains cut the tribe's domain into many small, widely scattered, self-contained communities; and certain cultural factors, such as the different dialects spoken in the three regional groupings, further discouraged any political cohesiveness. Even so, an occasional charismatic town chief in the early 1700s was able to exert influence beyond his own community. Such chiefs were better able to work with the colonists and traders from Carolina, who seemed to assume that all Cherokee towns constituted a single political entity that shared group responsibility for the action of any of its members.

Then, in 1721, Francis Nicholson, the royal governor of Carolina, persuaded Cherokee chiefs from thirty-seven towns to select one leader to represent them all in dealings relating to trade with Charleston. Nine years later, the English actually designated an "emperor" of the Cherokees, and soon thereafter tribal structures for punishing unauthorized actions by warriors began to appear. By the 1750s the initiative and energy of the council members of Chota contributed to the emergence of formal procedures, modeled after those of Cherokee town government, for formulating and implementing tribal policies.

Yet even this new national system proved inadequate for establishing a consensus among all of the elders of the tribe. Although the pressures resulting from sustained European contact encouraged the development of a national government, each town tended to follow the path of expediency. John Haywood, the early Tennessee historian, poignantly summarized the weaknesses of early eighteenth-century Cherokee tribal government:

> The king has neither guards, power, nor revenue. The council is no[t] otherwise respected than as their merit entitles them to it; and both may forfeit their rank and dignity by meanness and cowardice. None of the dignitaries, whether hereditary or raised to office by merit, must have any power contrary to the will of the nation. In every village there is a chief, or head, whose authority extends to his own tribe or family. Amongst the Cherokees, not only the king but the council is elective to supply deficiencies; though it is common to elevate the sons of any of the dignitaries to the rank of their fathers. The councils are attended by the whole nation, men, women and children. The progress of deliberation is frequently impeded, in order to consult the assembled nation. A few dissenting voices will often destroy the most salutary measures.

As one Cherokee chief explained, ''the people would work as they pleased and go to warr when they pleased, notwithstanding his saying all he could to them.''

In spite of particular differences, other Indians in Tennessee had local governments essentially similar to that of the Cherokees. All had town councils dominated by male elders and war organizations led by notable warriors. Unlike the Cherokees, however, these other tribes did not allow women to participate openly in politics. The political organization of all the Indian tribes was by European standards weak and ineffectual, with no real central authority or national power to coerce the autonomous towns to act in specific ways. Even within the towns there were limits to the coercive power of the local councils. The only real legal power resided with the clans.

The overriding principle of Indian law was retaliation, and the keeper of the law was the clan. An individual had legal rights primarily by virtue of his membership in a clan. Each clan was duly bound to revenge any wrongdoing perpetrated on one of its members. This rule especially applied to murder. The native peoples believed that a victim's spirit could not go to the next world until his death had been avenged. If the actual slayer could not be found and killed, one of the slayer's clansmen would be killed in his place. The fellow clansmen of the slayer were not supposed to interfere with the offended clan as it justly carried out its duty of killing the slayer. Nor did the slayer's own clan have any right to avenge their errant kinsman's death. This principle of noninterference was normally, though not always, adhered to, and thus perpetual blood feuds were usually avoided. In some cases an especially devoted relative of a slayer would volunteer to receive the death penalty in his kinsman's place. This happened more often when the offending act was manslaughter rather than murder, a distinction not necessarily made in Indian law.

To a large degree warfare was a further extension of the principle of retaliation, although other factors were involved, especially after the Indians became entangled with the European colonial powers. When used purely as a mechanism of revenge, Indian warfare was small in scale, involving skirmishes in which the loss of life was relatively low. For example, a Creek raiding party looking for trouble in Cherokee territory might surprise and kill a woman who had ventured out alone to fill a water jar at a stream. In revenge a Cherokee war party would travel down to Creek country where the warriors might encounter and kill two Creek hunters. The woman's death thus avenged, the Cherokees would return home victorious. The Creeks in turn might then retaliate by sending a raiding party back into Cherokee territory where the invaders might ambush some innocent individual such as an old man keeping crows away from a cornfield, perhaps killing him. And so it would go until the warring tribes grew weary of living in perpetual fear of each other or until some other circumstance induced them to arrange a peace. Peace emissaries would be sent by each tribe to the council houses of the other, and long, eloquent orations extolling the blessings of friendship and decrying the tragedy of war would be delivered by both sides.

Indian warfare, however, was not only a mechanism for revenge; it provided the primary means by which men gained status in these native societies. To accumulate more war honors, for instance, hot-headed young men often broke the peace between tribes.

The French and the English quickly learned to manipulate Indian warriors in the Europeans' own struggle for power in the Tennessee region. The colonial powers often found it to their advantage to stir up rivalries among the tribes. Not only did the French and English fight their wars through Indian allies, but the Europeans also encouraged these allies to fight among themselves, thus conveniently reducing the native population at every opportunity.

Although Indian warfare increased significantly under this outside influence, men seldom hurried off to war without first taking elaborate ritual precautions. They fasted and purified themselves and consulted with priests whom they believed could see into the future to tell them whether or not they would come back alive. If a negative sign was revealed to a warrior, he would withdraw from the raiding party and stay home. Once on the war trail, a warrior might watch for a warning in a dream or in the behavior of certain animals, particularly birds. Upon the appearance of such ill omens, individual warriors or even entire war parties might turn back and return home without any loss of face.

The Indians viewed most affairs having to do with themselves and the world around them in a spiritual context. They thought that most objects and occurrences in nature had spiritual counterparts. A Cherokee hunter, for example, who killed a deer without uttering the appropriate prayer of thanksgiving risked being hunted down by the Little White Deer, which was the spirit chief of the deer, and then being afflicted with arthritis. A lost child might be found and cared for and set on the path toward home by the Little People, knee-high spirit people who were at some times mischievous and at other times helpful. The Sun was the Indians' principal deity. Fire was its representative on earth, and Smoke was the messenger that bore prayers from the earth to heaven, where the Sun resided. The River was another powerful deity—among other things, it could help a man of knowledge divine the future.

Everything and every occurrence had natural and religious overtones for these people. Since no written native languages existed at that time, their beliefs, customs, traditions, and accumulated knowledge were transmitted orally to the young by the elders. Tales such as "How Day and Night were Divided" and "The Origin of Corn" reflect the efforts of the Indians to explain their physical universe in spiritual terms. Social themes and even human caricatures such as "The Wicked Mother-in-Law" also appeared in native folk tales.

The principal religious ceremony of Tennessee's Indians, except for the Shawnees, was the annual Green Corn Ceremony. This harvest celebration, called the *boosketah* ("to fast") by the Creeks, occurred at the beginning of the corn harvest. During this observance, the Indians extinguished the town's sacred fire and rekindled a new one to signify the birth of a new year. The ceremony also represented the Indians' quest for purity. Following a two-day fast, for example, the Chickasaws drank a bitter beverage made from boiled cusseena, button snakeroot, or red root that caused them to vomit, thus purging themselves of the physical and spiritual impurities in their bodies. Following this purification ritual, they joined in a feast of roasting corn.

In addition to its religious overtones, the Green Corn Ceremony also had a deep moral significance. Tribal elders warned their assembled people that the health and prosperity of everyone depended on the virtue of each individual, that the sins of one person could bring misfortune to all. Indian children listened attentively to such lectures, as well as to those on tribal traditions and lore.

The Green Corn Ceremony was also a time for straightening out any social relationships that had become disordered in the course of the past year. During the celebrations, all crimes except murder were pardoned. And other offenders, such as adulterers, who had managed to hide from their avengers could return home without fear during this period. Although peace and friendship represented a dominant theme of the observance, the Indians took the opportunity to promote military virtues as well. Warriors advanced to a higher rank, and young men who had won distinction in battle received appropriate recognition for their deeds.

Among the Shawnees in the Cumberland River Valley, the annual Green Corn Ceremony was more a time of fun and frolic than of sacred rituals and solemnity. Much more significant to the Shawnees was their Bread Dance which began the festivities of the spring. Not until this important celebration was concluded would any Shawnee venture to plant a crop or start any other important undertaking. During the Bread Dance, the Shawnees asked *Moneto*, their Supreme Being, to bless the people, to provide them with a bountiful crop, and to give them a peaceful and prosperous year.

Many of these customs and beliefs persisted long after the introduction of western European culture to the Tennessee area. Indian-white contact led neither to the complete adoption of European ways by the natives nor to the assimilation of the Indians into colonial society. Nevertheless, the traditional native way of life was severely eroded, leaving the Indians vulnerable to the considerable pressure exerted upon them by the Europeans. By the eighteenth century the Indians found themselves too much dependent on European trade goods and alliances to pursue their own interests without regard to the wishes of colonial allies. Native societies increasingly became more disrupted. Their numbers were steadily reduced by European diseases and perpetual warfare. By 1840, three centuries after de Soto entered Tennessee, the only Indians still remaining in the region were a small number of Cherokees who found themselves almost completely disinherited from their ancestral domain.

3. The Creeks and the Shawnees

The Creeks and the Shawnees played their most decisive role in Tennessee history at a time when they no longer lived in the area.

There were never many Creeks living in Tennessee; the few settlements that did exist were in the vicinity of present-day Chattanooga, with perhaps a small number of other enclaves located farther up the Tennessee River. By 1715, however, their traditional enemies, the powerful Cherokees, forced the Creeks in East Tennessee to abandon the area. English colonials in Charleston had deliberately fomented war between the Cherokees and the Creeks in order to obtain Indian slaves to sell in the West Indies. Charleston slave traders clandestinely supplied both sides with weapons and ammunition on the condition that the natives turn over to them all prisoners taken in battle. Thus, the guns and ammunition supplied by the slave traders enabled the Cherokees to wage war against the Creeks and force them to move south.

The Shawnees were likewise expelled from the Tennessee area by other Indians. During the early eighteenth century, Shawnee hunting parties and villages in the Cumberland River Valley of Middle Tennessee and Kentucky increasingly came under attack from other Indians. This area was abundant with game, and by 1715 French traders were operating a trading post near the present site of Nashville. The post was close to the Cumberland River, which was then called by the French the *Chaouanon*, or "Shawnee" River. By this time the fur trade had become a lucrative business for the French as the Shawnees and other tribes brought in large numbers of pelts to exchange for European goods. The Chickasaws, moving in from the west, were especially aggressive in their attacks on the Shawnees. But numerous other Indians also claimed hunting privileges in the valley area, including the Creeks from below the big bend of the Tennessee River, the Cherokees from the east and the south, and the mighty Iroquois, among others, from the north. So fierce was the competition for control of the area that it became known by the Indians as "the Dark and Bloody Ground."

There were many conflicts along the Indian trails in Middle Tennessee and numerous "canoe fights" on the Cumberland River whenever Shawnee hunting parties accidentally encountered Creek, Chickasaw, Cherokee, or Iroquois hunting bands. According to the French Canadian, Jean du Charleville, who worked at the French trading post, a large body of Chickasaws ambushed a Shawnee hunting party in 1710. The Chickasaws hid on both sides of the Cumberland River at a location just a short distance above the mouth of the Harpeth River. They ferociously attacked the unsuspecting Shawnees, killing most of them and the trader who accompanied them and stealing all of their animal pelts and other goods. In 1715 the Cherokees, who were as eager as the Chickasaws to hunt in the Cumberland River Valley, united with the Chickasaws to drive the Shawnees out of the area. While some of the fugitive Shawnee bands turned south to join the Creeks in Alabama, most of them had settled north of the Ohio River by 1730.

The Shawnees did not completely abandon the Tennessee region, however. Small parties of these Indians frequently returned to the Cumberland River Valley to hunt. Once again, in 1745, the Chickasaws and the Cherokees united to remove the Shawnee intruders from the hunting lands near the future site of Nashville. The Shawnees fleeing the Cumberland Valley migrated along a circuitous route through Kentucky and eventually settled in Ohio. A band which had previously settled with the Creeks to the south of the Tennessee region apparently moved into the Cumberland area after the mid-eighteenth century, but it too was ejected by the Chickasaws, this time unassisted by the Cherokees.

As a result of their numerous migrations, the Shawnees forged many alliances with other tribes. Their wanderings and alliances, together with their constant guerrilla warfare against the advancing tide of white settlement, made the Shawnee people extremely conscious of the need for Indian unity against the Americans. The need must have been especially apparent to Tecumseh, the younger brother of the Shawnee warrior Cheeseekau, for Tecumseh would later give his life in pursuit of that cause—a united front against the white settlers.

In the wooded hills and valleys of Tennessee and Kentucky where the Shawnees continued to hunt, frontiersmen feared and hated them for their depredations against white settlements. During and after the American Revolutionary War, Shawnee warriors like Cheeseekau often joined forces with the Chickamaugans—a collection of disgruntled Cherokees, Creeks, and white Tories under the leadership of the Cherokee warrior Dragging Canoe—to terrorize settlers in the Cumberland River Valley. In the late 1780s Cheeseekau joined the Chickamaugans at their Running Water Town headquarters on the south bank of the Tennessee River near present-day Chattanooga. Several years later, he urged Tecumseh to join him. Tecumseh, whose parents had once lived in Middle Tennessee, journeyed south with a band of Shawnee warriors to join his brother. On one of their raids against the Cumberland settlements in 1792, Cheeseekau was killed. Tecumseh, burying Cheeseekau's body in a secret grave, vowed to avenge his brother's death.

The Shawnee warriors selected Tecumseh, then only about twenty-four years of age, to succeed Cheeseekau as their leader. During the following months Tecumseh and his contingent of Shawnees fought alongside the Chickamaugans, taking part in a series of raids and fierce skirmishes against settlers in Tennessee and adjoining areas. In September 1794, frontier militia under Major James Ore burned two Chickamaugan towns, including Running Water Town, and Chickamaugan resistance ended shortly thereafter. Before this time Tecumseh had returned north to defend the Ohio country against an invasion by a Federal army under Major-General Anthony Wayne, but his experiences among the fierce Chickamaugans helped him shape a plan for protecting the rights of all Indian people. Tecumseh envisioned the establishment of an intertribal confederacy to stop American encroachments on Indian lands. He now set about to make his dream a reality.

In the 1790s the Cherokees and the Chickasaws were the only tribes that the United States government recognized as owning land in the Tennessee region, a fact that ignored the Shawnees and the Creeks who claimed hunting privileges in the Cumberland River Valley. When the Chickamaugan towns fell to the white militia in 1794, fleeing Creek warriors vowed that they would "be at war with the Cumberland people the longest day they would have to live on account of the land." This threat of Creek aggression and the settlers' need to strike first was in fact cited a short time earlier as a reason for Tennessee statehood. On August 25, 1794, in the first published statement calling for formation of the new state, the *Knoxville Gazette* put this question to its readers:

> Would it not be wise in the approaching General Assembly, to take measures that this Territory may, as speedily as possible, become a member state of the federal union? The people would then, by their immediate representatives, have a right to vote upon the important question of peace or war against that sanguinary nation (the Creeks) whose thirst for blood appears insatiable. Not a month, rarely a week has elapsed for ten years past, without some defenceless frontier family having fallen victims to their savage barbarity.

(*Above*): Sketch of the Shawnee warrior Tecumseh during the War of 1812 based on an earlier drawing by a French trader. Courtesy of National Anthropological Archives, Smithsonian Institution. (*Below*): An artist's depiction of the massacre by the Creek Red Sticks at Fort Mims, 1813. Courtesy of Alabama Department of Archives and History.

Following Tennessee's admission to statehood in 1796, President George Washington sent North Carolinian Benjamin Hawkins to the Creek country in what is today Alabama and Georgia to promote peace on the southern frontier by the ''proper management'' of these Indians. During the next fifteen years while Indian agent Hawkins endeavored to refashion Creek government, society, and subsistence patterns in the American image, there arose a group of native leaders who steadfastly resisted these efforts. These men were receptive to the teachings of Tecumseh.

Tecumseh had close ties with the Creeks. Although his father was a Shawnee, his mother was a Creek, and in the Creeks' matrilineal view of things that made Tecumseh a brother. So as Tecumseh developed his plan to unite the various tribes against white encroachment, he traveled to the Creek country in 1811 and used his passionate eloquence to enlist them in his cause. The majority of Creeks by this time had resigned themselves to living alongside the Americans and thus turned a deaf ear to Tecumseh. But there were many among the Creeks who wanted no part of the white man's civilization, and they paid close attention to Tecumseh's ''talks.'' These militant Creeks became known as the ''Red Sticks'' after Tecumseh supposedly gave their leaders bundles of sticks painted red to count the days until the time of the planned concerted uprising.

Tecumseh's visit to the Creek country was part of an extensive recruiting campaign among the southern tribes that he had begun earlier. The Shawnee warrior had journeyed down the Ohio and Mississippi rivers to the present site of Memphis. From there he traveled to Indian settlements in Mississippi, Alabama, Georgia, and Florida before heading back north through Georgia to the Carolinas and then across Tennessee to the Ozark Mountains of Arkansas and Missouri. Wherever he went, Tecumseh's message was the same. The Indian tribes must abandon the white man's practices and his goods, and they must return to their old ways. He warned that the white settlers, if not pushed away, would seize all Indian lands and enslave or exterminate the tribes. All southern native peoples, he continued, should join forces with the Shawnees, their northern Indian allies, and the English king in a holy war against the American encroachers. As Tecumseh spoke, according to an observer, ''his eyes burned with supernatural lustre, and his whole frame trembled with emotion: his voice resounded over the multitude—now sinking in low and musical whispers, now rising to its highest key, hurling out his words like a succession of thunderbolts.'' Although most chiefs tried to temper the passions of their people, Tecumseh continued to make some converts nearly everywhere he spoke.

The Chickasaws listened to the counsel of their American agent, James Robertson, and rejected Tecumseh's overtures. Mixed blood leader George

Colbert, a personal friend of agent Robertson, told the Shawnee leader that the Chickasaws were at peace with the Americans and would not undertake any actions that might lead to war and, as a possible result, the loss of some tribal land.

Undaunted by the refusal of aid from the Chickasaws, Tecumseh tried to persuade the Cherokees, and for that purpose he met their chiefs at Soco Gap, in the Balsom range of the Great Smoky Mountains. Again Tecumseh was rebuffed; the Cherokees had fought the Americans during the Revolutionary War and for several years thereafter, yet now they too were reluctant to take up arms against their white neighbors. The decision of the leaders at the Soco Gap parley was confirmed by council meetings elsewhere in the Cherokee settlements. Thus, among the Chickasaws and Cherokees, the only tribes still possessing land within the present boundaries of Tennessee, Tecumseh had made little headway.

Tecumseh did find converts elsewhere, and even supernatural forces seemed to be on his side. The Shawnee warrior had promised the Creeks that when he returned to the North he would signal the start of the holy war by stamping his foot on the ground and causing the earth to tremble. A comet, a shower of meteors, and some tremendous earthquakes occurred thereafter which gave added weight to his pronouncements. Between December 1811 and February 1812 a series of earthquakes struck the western frontier with such force that the resulting shock waves destroyed the town of New Madrid in the Missouri Territory and possibly caused a portion of the Mississippi River to flow backwards for a short time. As Indian houses began to shake and pottery knocked together, many skeptics succumbed to the belief that Tecumseh did have great medicine with which to push the Americans into the sea. The Red Sticks prepared for victory.

During the War of 1812, while Tecumseh was away gathering warriors from northern tribes to fight against the Americans, the Red Sticks launched scattered attacks against the southern frontier. Indignation and cries for revenge swept Middle Tennessee when a Creek raiding party killed seven people in a surprise attack on a settlement near the mouth of the Duck River and immediately withdrew with an American woman as a prisoner. The Tennessee state legislature, in outrage at the "horrid and inhuman" murders committed by the Creeks, called for proper "atonements." White Tennesseans agreed with the frontier editor who warned, "When the tomahawk and the scalping knife are drawn in the cabins of our peaceful and unsuspecting citizens[,] it is time, high time to prepare at least for defense." The murders and thefts committed by the Red Sticks brought angry demands for vengeance throughout the frontier.

Andrew Jackson prepared to raise a force of volunteers to retaliate against the Creeks and to rescue the captured woman, but Governor Willie Blount informed him that he could not act without approval from the War Department. Jackson was indignant. Like other Tennesseans, including Governor Blount, he had hoped that the current struggle with England would make possible the merging of the Indian problem on the southern frontier with the conduct of the war. But his hands were tied. Then on August 30, 1813, about 1,000 Red Stick warriors including the influential mixed blood leader William Weatherford struck at Fort Mims, a few miles above Mobile in Alabama, killing and scalping large numbers of men, women, and children. Estimates of the number murdered range from over 200 to more than 500.

Weatherford's participation in the Fort Mims massacre provides some insights into the fratricidal strife that was tearing the Creek Nation apart in the early 1800s. At the time of the attack, Weatherford—called Red Eagle by the Creeks—was about thirty-three years old. Although his father was a Scottish trader and his brother lived among the whites, he had long ago chosen to live with his mother's Creek kin. Inspired by the "talks" of Tecumseh, Red Eagle sympathized with those Creek leaders who opposed the efforts of American agent Benjamin Hawkins to transform them into images of white people.

Following Tecumseh's strategy, Red Eagle hoped to participate in a war between the Creeks and whites. But he found himself facing the prospect of participating in a Creek civil war. Indeed, a number of mixed blood supporters of the Americans, including some of Red Eagle's relatives and acquaintances, had taken refuge at Fort Mims before the Red Stick attack. Red Eagle contemplated abandoning the war party, but some of the warriors seized his family and black slaves as hostages to assure his cooperation. This action prompted his decision to join the attack on Fort Mims. Although he became an important leader of the assault, he tried to convince the warriors to spare the lives of the women and children. His efforts to stop the carnage failed and, in order to disassociate himself from the butchery that was taking place, he left the fort. Red Eagle fully recognized the consequences of the massacre, however, and joined his Red Stick brethren in the ensuing war against the whites and their Indian allies.

The news of the bloody massacre at Fort Mims spread fear in every white settlement on the southern frontier. In Knoxville, the Tennessee General

---

(*Above*): General Andrew Jackson's victories over the Red Sticks and at the battle of New Orleans made him a national hero. Courtesy of Tennessee Conservation Department. (*Below*): An old engraving portrays Red Eagle surrendering to General Andrew Jackson. Courtesy of Alabama Department of Archives and History.

Assembly promptly empowered Governor Blount to call for volunteers to punish the Red Sticks. General Jackson, in command of one of the two armies of Tennessee volunteers and militia, quickly started out on a retaliatory mission against the belligerent Creeks. During approximately the same period, in October 1813, American soldiers to the north killed Tecumseh at the battle of the Thames in Canada; the news of Tecumseh's death crushed the spirit of the northern Indians. Now Jackson hoped to subdue the hostile southern Indians as well. He would defeat the Red Sticks by burning their towns and plundering their supplies.

Jackson's soldiers were accompanied by contingents of "loyal" Indians including Creek warriors led by mixed blood chief William McIntosh. The number of hostile Indian dead left behind by the advancing troops, according to Jackson himself, adequately revenged the Fort Mims massacre. David Crockett, who took part in the fighting, later admitted that the Tennessee volunteers had shot the Red Sticks "like dogs." After one battle, however, General Jackson saved a Creek child's life and later took the boy, named Lincoya, back to the Hermitage in Nashville where he raised him as his son. But despite Jackson's show of kindness to this child, he remained ruthless in his military campaign. At last, on March 27, 1814, his soldiers and Indian allies defeated the Red Sticks by killing more than 800 of their best warriors at Horseshoe Bend on the Tallapoosa River in Alabama.

After this victory, Jackson pursued a scorched-earth policy until, out of sheer desperation, the last of the renegade Creek leaders including Red Eagle surrendered. Red Eagle is alleged to have walked into Jackson's camp and to have addressed the general in this manner:

> General Jackson, I am not afraid of you. I fear no man, for I am a Creek warrior. I have nothing to request in behalf of myself; you can kill me if you desire. But I come to beg you to send for the women and children of the war party, who are now starving in the woods. Their fields and cribs have been destroyed by your people, who have driven them to the woods without an ear of corn. I hope that you will send out parties who will safely conduct them here, in order that they may be fed. I exerted myself in vain to prevent the massacre of the women and children at Fort Mims. I am now done fighting. The Red Sticks are nearly all killed. If I could fight you any longer I would most heartily do so. Send for the women and children. They never did you any harm. But kill me, if the white people want it done.

Jackson, so the story goes, was so moved by the words of his foe that he extended his hand and offered to feed the Red Stick women and children. Although some historians have challenged the authenticity of this dramatic surrender speech, it is known that Red Eagle surrendered to Jackson and that the general allowed him to return to his home in Alabama. There was no longer any need to fear Red Eagle or the other Red Stick leaders. On the southern frontier as well as in the Old Northwest, the Indian resistance to white expansion, inspired by the words of Tecumseh, appeared to be over.

Thus, nearly a century after the Chickasaws and the Cherokees had first expelled the Shawnees and the Creeks from the Tennessee region, American soldiers in 1813 at the battle of the Thames and in 1814 at the battle of Horseshoe Bend took the final steps to guarantee that these ejected peoples would never again return to their ancestral land in Tennessee. Tecumseh's death in 1813 broke the spirit of his people. There were no more Shawnee-inspired raids on the Cumberland settlements. General Jackson's victory over the Red Sticks in 1814 allowed him to force a treaty on the entire Creek Nation for the actions of the warring minority. Jackson demanded twenty-three million acres of Creek land—approximately two-thirds of their territory, amounting to three-fifths of Alabama and one-fifth of Georgia. Tennesseans hailed him as a hero for removing the Creek Indians from land adjacent to their state's borders, for opening new land to settlement, and for securing a stretch of land for a broad and open road to the Gulf of Mexico.

For the Creeks the Treaty of 1814 marked the beginning of a series of land confiscations that left them in such a demoralized state by the mid-1830s that they resorted to stealing, arson, and eventually murder in order to survive. Andrew Jackson, then President of the United States, forced the Creeks and the other southern Indians to emigrate across the Mississippi River. In the trans-Mississippi West the people of the Creek Confederacy, whose grand alliance had dominated the South for hundreds of years, found themselves strangers in a new land which they and numerous other Indian peoples now came to know as Indian Territory.

4. The Chickasaws

The Chickasaws first encountered Europeans when the Spanish force under Hernando de Soto, after leaving East Tennessee and fighting its way out of Alabama, entered the Chickasaw domain in northern Mississippi in late December 1540. One hundred and fifty years after de Soto's visit, the French, coming down the Mississippi River, and the English, entering Tennessee from the east, found the Chickasaws living in basically the same area where de Soto had encountered them. The English and the French would ultimately have a great and disruptive influence on the lives of these Indian people who claimed all of the western region and part of the middle section of Tennessee as their hunting grounds.

By the close of the seventeenth century, European traders began establishing themselves among the Chickasaws. As the number of traders increased, so did their influence on tribal life. European trading houses gradually displaced the council houses as the center of tribal affairs. Traders married native women, who bore their children, giving rise to a mixed blood population with ties to both the Indian's and the white man's worlds.

European trade goods seemed in the short view to make life simpler for the Chickasaw people. Their warriors found the guns, knives, and hatchets of the English to be highly desirable weapons for hunting as well as for battle. The Indians also prized English brass wire for making bracelets and earrings. Chickasaw women obtained such useful implements as iron hoes to cultivate their crops more easily and iron axes to facilitate the gathering of firewood. English textiles provided more attractive and comfortable clothes for their families. The English traders from Carolina were able to offer cheaper and more abundant trade goods than were their French counterparts. Thus, lured by a greater return on the animal pelts and Indian slaves given in payment to the traders, the Chickasaw people aligned themselves with Carolina against her enemies.

One result of the growing addiction of the Chickasaws and their neighbors to European trade goods was the intensification of Indian competition for hunting grounds which resulted in hostilities that provided a greatly increased number of native captives. Although the Indians had enslaved members of their own race before European contact, the high value placed on native slaves by the Carolina traders, who shipped them to the West Indies, induced Chickasaw warriors to raid their neighbors for slaves even when hunting grounds were not at issue. After the introduction of the horse, Chickasaw slave-raiding parties ranged far and wide; such parties even ventured west of the Mississippi River and north of the Ohio River.

The English were also responsible for introducing Negro slavery to the Chickasaw people. The first blacks in the tribal domain were the servants of English traders, but slaveholding by the Indians themselves grew rapidly, especially among the mixed bloods like the Colbert family. The Colberts were the offspring of a Scottish father, who came to the tribe in 1729, and his three native wives. With their attractive homes and hundreds of black slaves, the Colberts were the principal spokesmen for the tribe for over a century, and they also set the economic and social tone for mixed blood emulation. By the early nineteenth century these mixed bloods controlled tribal affairs, and the Chickasaw people had become intensely dedicated slaveholders. European modes had gradually replaced Indian ways, just as European consumer goods had altered traditional self-sufficiency of this native people.

In the Colonial period, European traders in the Chickasaw country proved to be the vanguard of European troops, fortifications, and settlements. Competition among colonial powers for political and economic supremacy in the region led to a long and bloody contest for control of the lower Mississippi Valley. During this struggle, which lasted nearly a century, both the English and the French used the Chickasaws as pawns.

The Chickasaws were not so immersed in the European wars of empire as to neglect their own immediate interests, however. For example, on two different occasions (1715 and 1745) in the fight over the hunting grounds of Middle Tennessee, they had combined forces with the Cherokees to expel the Shawnees from that area. And later, in 1769, when the Cherokees challenged the eastward movement of the Chickasaws onto lands in Middle Tennessee that the Cherokees themselves claimed, the Chickasaws soundly defeated their former allies. Yet in spite of the independence they showed in dealing with other native peoples, the Chickasaws found themselves coming more and more under European influence.

Once the British secured title in 1763 to the area between the Atlantic Ocean and the Mississippi River, Chickasaw-white contact accelerated rapidly and the mixed blood population increased. The avenue to tribal leadership shifted from clan leaders known for their wisdom or bravery to mixed bloods who sought accommodation with the emerging new order and thus were able to deal more effectively with the whites. Out of deference to the

full bloods who made up three-fourths of the tribal population, the mixed bloods preserved the old system of a hereditary principal chief, or *High Minko*, and the council of clan chiefs. But the real power in Chickasaw politics resided with the mixed bloods who emulated the planters and traders in the British colonies. Some full bloods, however, like war chief Piomingo, desperately sought to retain the old ways.

Piomingo and other traditionalists viewed the European traders as disruptive forces in tribal life. These full blood leaders particularly protested against the rum dealers who lurked in the woods enticing Chickasaw hunters to sample their wares and then cheated them out of their animal pelts when the Indians were thoroughly drunk. Despite repeated complaints from their leaders, however, most full bloods were as dependent on the traders as were the mixed bloods.

When the American Revolutionary War broke out, the majority of the Chickasaws sided with England, no doubt because of their long-time allegiance to the British as well as their desire to protect their territory from the land-hungry colonists. In the view of Virginia Governor Thomas Jefferson the Chickasaws were in fact the key to British defenses south of the Ohio River, and he hoped to bring these natives under American control. As a first step, he ordered Colonel George Rogers Clark of the Virginia militia to construct a fort below the mouth of the Ohio River in Indian territory. Completed in April 1780 and garrisoned with 100 soldiers, Fort Jefferson stood on the east bank of the Mississippi River about four miles below the mouth of the Ohio River near present-day Columbus, Kentucky. The Chickasaws harassed the fort with continual raids, however, until in June 1781 the colonials finally abandoned the location. Their retreat effectively ended Jefferson's plan to invade the British stronghold in the Old Southwest. Meanwhile, a group of English soldiers threw in with the Chickasaws and under the leadership of James Colbert continued to raid white settlements. Crude buildings erected at the Lower Chickasaw Bluffs, near the site of present-day Memphis, served as their base of operations. From here the Chickasaws struck at outposts as far away as the Cumberland River Valley.

Frontiersmen had begun settling the Cumberland River Valley in an organized fashion near the end of 1779. Their move was sponsored by the Transylvania Company, organized a few years earlier by Judge Richard Henderson of North Carolina who had purchased this land from the Chero-

---

These are examples of the trade goods that Europeans used as currency in the fur trade. From Lewis and Kneberg, *Tribes That Slumber: Indians of the Tennessee Region.*

kees. In the vanguard of the Cumberland settlers was James Robertson, sometimes referred to as the "Father of Tennessee." Robertson led an overland expedition from the Watauga settlements in 1779 and built Fort Nashborough, the future site of Nashville, on the western bank of the Cumberland River. The settlers who accompanied Robertson were soon joined by additional families who arrived in April 1780 in a flotilla of flatboats under the command of John Donelson. By late spring several hundred people were living in scattered settlements along the river. The growth of these settlements and the construction of Fort Jefferson during that same period were regarded by the Chickasaws as acts of aggression, and they retaliated. As Indian raids increased, the frontiersmen banded together on May 1, 1780, to form the "Cumberland Compact," a temporary government and a voluntary association to protect their lives and property from such attacks. Nevertheless, the Chickasaws and other tribes from both sides of the Ohio River continued to harass the Cumberland outposts.

As the American Revolutionary War drew to a close, the Chickasaw people found it necessary to re-evaluate their attitude toward the Cumberland settlers. British withdrawal from the lower Mississippi Valley brought disunity to the tribe. The American and Spanish governments, allies in the war against England, now vied for treaties of alliance with the Indians. One tribal faction, led by Piomingo, favored the Americans, partly because the white settlers were so much like the Indians' old English ally and partly because the Piomingo forces feared an attack by northern tribes, which the Spanish incited against the Chickasaws during the recent war.

During the spring and summer of 1782, the Chickasaws made overtures for peace. The tribe was in an unenviable position at this time. Spanish and American officials were demanding treaties of alliance. Indians in the Old Northwest were threatening war, surveyors from the Cumberland settlements were in the tribal hunting territory, and Virginians were asking for a land cession. To make matters worse, the Chickasaws were uncertain as to who actually represented the new American government. Although the new nation's Articles of Confederation claimed the power of "regulating the trade and managing all affairs" with the Indians, agents from Virginia and other

---

(*Above*): James Robertson urged Cumberland settlers to court the Chickasaws as an ally against other hostile tribes. Courtesy of Tennessee State Museum. (*Below*): Indian treaty cessions in Tennessee (conflicting Chickasaw claims with Cherokee claims east of the Tennessee River were removed by treaties in 1805 and 1816). Based on map in J. Leonard Raulston and James W. Livingood, *Sequatchie: A Story of the Southern Cumberlands.*

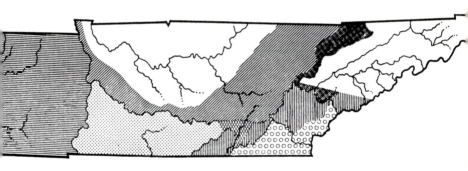

 Pre-Statehood Treaties, 1770–91

First Treaty of Tellico, 1798

Third Treaty of Tellico, 1805

Dearborn's Treaty, 1806

 Jackson and McMinn Treaty, 1817

Jackson Purchase Treaty, 1818

Calhoun's Treaty, 1819

Treaty of New Echota, 1835

southern states were carrying on their own negotiations with the tribes.
Through the English interpreter residing in the Chickasaw Nation, Piomingo
wrote American military officials that "what damage Was done [to you by the
Chickasaws] was by Reason [that] you Settled A Fort in Our Hunting ground
without Our Leave." Hoping to make amends for previous acts of hostility
against the settlements, Piomingo and other members of his faction claimed
that "the English put the Bloody Tomahawk into our hands, telling us that we
should have no Goods if we did not Exert ourselves to the greatest point of
Resentment against you, but now we find our mistake and Distresses."

James Robertson, the recognized leader of the Cumberland settlers, was
anxious to win the Chickasaws over to the American side. An alliance with
this tribe would provide the frontiersmen with a valuable ally against the
Creeks and the Cherokees, who continued to pillage American outposts, and
would help prevent occupation of the strategic Chickasaw Bluffs by a European nation. In December 1782, therefore, Robertson established a supply
depot for the Chickasaws at the Lower Bluff, and the Cumberland settlers
began sending gifts and trade goods to the members of the tribe stationed
there. Meanwhile, Virginia Governor Benjamin Harrison, who was eager to
take advantage of Piomingo's conciliatory attitude, sent John Donelson and
Joseph Martin to Nashborough to negotiate a treaty with the Chickasaws.

Both the Chickasaws and the frontiersmen benefited from the resulting
Chickasaw-Virginia Treaty of 1783. Virginia agreed to assist the natives in
preventing the passage of whites through their lands, to help eject intruders
form the tribal domain (in return for the Chickasaws' promise to free settlers
held captive), and to aid in expelling any Europeans among them hostile to
American independence. The most significant aspect of the treaty negotiations, however, was that the Virginia commissioners were unable to secure a
land cession from the Indians.

The Chickasaw-Virginia Treaty was only a preliminary step to comprehen-
sive negotiations with the Indians by the American government. Two years
later, the Continental Congress, fearful that Spain was making headway
among the southern tribes, appointed commissioners to secure treaties of
friendship with them. The commissioners opened negotiations in late 1785 at
a place called Hopewell on the Keowee River in South Carolina, and during
the ensuing winter they concluded treaties with the Cherokees, Choctaws, and
Chickasaws. The treaty with the Chickasaws, signed on January 10, 1786,
marked the beginning of official relations between the tribe and the new
American nation. Although William Blount, a land speculator who was North
Carolina's agent at the proceedings, hoped to obtain a boundary line on the
Tennessee River, the commissioners recognized the tribe's claim in what is

today Tennessee to include part of the middle section as well as all of the western region of the state. Another clause in the treaty, probably little understood by the full bloods, provided that the American government "for the benefit and comfort of the Indians . . . shall have the sole and exclusive right of regulating the trade with the Indians, and managing all their affairs."

Following the signing of this treaty, the Chickasaw people found themselves caught up in the competitive struggle between Spain and the United States for control of the lower Mississippi Valley, with each side trying to strengthen its position by courting the tribe. American trade goods and weapons destined for the Chickasaws—to keep them loyal to the United States—were flowing southwesterly on the Ohio and Mississippi for distribution at Chickasaw Bluffs. In the summer of 1792, William Blount, who President George Washington had appointed governor and Indian superintendent for the Territory South of the River Ohio two years earlier, met with Piomingo and other leaders of the tribe in a further effort to curb Spanish influence. Blount succeeded in securing a treaty of peace and friendship with the Chickasaws, at a council held near present-day Nashville, after assuring the tribal leaders that, contrary to Spanish claims, the United States had no designs on their land. In conducting relations with one another the Chickasaw and American allies sometimes traveled on an old Indian trail known as the Chickasaw Trace (later called the Natchez Trace). The trail extended in a southwesterly direction from today's Nashville to the center of the Chickasaw Nation near Tupelo, Mississippi, and then on through much of Mississippi to Natchez.

Piomingo's treaty with the Americans proved costly for his tribe. Chickasaw warriors returning from the North, where they had helped Major-General Anthony Wayne achieve victory against hostile Indians at Fallen Timbers in 1794, were attacked viciously by a white mob in Cincinnati. In addition to being clubbed and stoned, as they were in Cincinnati, by citizens of the same government they had supported in battle at Fallen Timbers, the Chickasaws were encountering other difficulties. The Creek Indians, allies of the Spanish, were raiding Chickasaw villages and ambushing their hunters along the trails leading to the Tennessee and Cumberland rivers. This Creek-Chickasaw conflict elicited strong sympathy for the Chickasaws from frontier residents such as William C. C. Claiborne who observed:

> They are a small people, and if left to themselves, must fall a sacrifice to the numerous Creeks—Honor, justice and gratitude, call upon the Americans to assist them; but if the dictates of these social virtues of the heart, are not listened to—policy requires that America should preserve that nation; they serve as a barrier between the settlement of Cumberland, and the hostile

Indian tribes; and should the Chickasaws fall (if Congress pursues the same conduct towards us, as heretofore, to wit, that of affording us no protection) the Cumberland settlement must fall also.

By the end of 1795 the Spanish-supported Creeks sued for peace with the Chickasaws when, thanks in large measure to the Pinckney Treaty with Spain, the United States won the contest for the control of the lower Mississippi Valley.

Domination of the region by the United States meant that the Americans no longer had to make promises to the Chickasaws to lure them away from foreign adversaries. As a result, the history of these people after 1795 is a chronicle of continuing land cessions extracted from the tribe to satisfy the voracious appetites of white settlers and speculators. The Indian population was increasingly concentrated on a diminishing land base.

Even the popularity of the Natchez Trace contributed to the white pressure on the Chickasaws. As early as 1797, the American government began delivering the mail between Nashville and the Mississippi River town of Natchez along this old Indian trail that lay within the Chickasaw domain. In 1801 at a treaty session held at Chickasaw Bluffs, Brigadier-General James Wilkerson bribed George Colbert, the mixed blood spokesman for the assembled Indian chiefs, to gain approval for the United States to "lay out, open and make a convenient wagon road through their land . . . for the citizens of the United States, and the Chickasaws." The treaty committed the Indians to keep this road, the Natchez Trace, open at all times. It became the most heavily traveled road in the Old Southwest, another factor aiding the establishment of white settlements, and the Chickasaws came under strong pressure to permit the construction of additional roads through their territory.

In the early 1800s, economic distress in the American East brought a flood of settlers into the Tennessee region, many of them eager to settle in the Chickasaw domain. In order to accommodate his countrymen's wishes, President Thomas Jefferson advised government Indian agents to encourage the Chickasaws to buy goods from government trading houses so that they would "run in debt beyond their individual means of paying; and, whenever in that situation, they will always cede lands to rid themselves of debt." In accordance with the President's wishes, Congress provided for the establishment of a government trading house near Fort Pickering on the Lower Chickasaw Bluffs in 1802. The Indians used these bluffs on the Mississippi River, more than 100 miles distant from their principal towns in what is now the state of Mississippi, as a port to meet supply boats and to barter with traders. The new trading house soon attracted large numbers of Chickasaws. In 1809, according to Lieutenant Zachary Taylor, the Indians had a large settlement about five miles inland from the Mississippi River. A smaller group, less than fifty members of the tribe and their slaves, resided in a temporary village located on the elevated river bed at the base of the Lower Bluffs. Included with this village were three or four corn fields and a quarter-mile race track where the Chickasaws tested the speed of their ponies. At the trading house, government officials followed Jefferson's plan to gain further land cessions by encouraging the Indians to run into debt.

The Chickasaws brought ever larger numbers of animal pelts, mostly deer, to the trading house. This establishment was well supplied with goods and was quite liberal in extending credit. United States officials had learned that a good line of merchandise was necessary because, as the manager of the trading house reported in 1808, "no people are more particular or more suspicious than the Chickasaws." But if the quality of the goods was high, so too were the prices. Each year during that period, the Chickasaws incurred debts amounting to several thousands of dollars for such miscellaneous items as rifles, gun powder, lanterns, rings, blankets, sheets, calico, saddles, and shoes. Within a short time the American government possessed the lever necessary to pry loose more Chickasaw land.

Between 1805 and 1818 General Andrew Jackson and other treaty commissioners used threats, economic coercion, and bribery to extinguish Indian title to nearly twenty million acres of land and to open vital lines of communication lying within the tribal domain. In 1805, the Chickasaws ceded to the United States a section of their domain northeast of the Tennessee River, composed mostly of a large tract of land in Middle Tennessee, in exchange for a cancellation of a $12,000 debt. Despite the economic coercion that produced this cession, the Chickasaws reaffirmed their loyalty to the United States during the War of 1812 by providing fighting men for the American army in the campaign against the Creek Red Sticks. One year after the battle of New Orleans, General Jackson "rewarded" them for their assistance: in 1816, Jackson and his fellow commissioners saw to it that the Chickasaws lost tribal title to all land on the northeast side of the Tennessee River, including a large southwestern portion of Middle Tennessee. After the Treaty of 1816, the only land remaining to the Chickasaws within the Tennessee region was in West Tennessee. Two years later, this too would belong to the United States.

In the spring of 1818 the Tennessee General Assembly petitioned Congress to erase Chickasaw title to all land remaining within the borders of the state. The spread of cotton cultivation following the invention of the cotton gin in 1793 and a rising anxiety over the question of state sovereignty in the area claimed by the Chickasaws had led the assembly to take this action. Congress, anxious to evict the Indians from their hunting grounds in the strategic Ohio and Mississippi River valleys, promptly appointed General Jackson and Isaac Shelby, the former governor of Kentucky, as treaty commissioners. Washing-

ton officials wanted to create a buffer zone between the southern Indians and
those in the Old Northwest so as to prevent another native leader like
Tecumseh from attempting to unify the tribes against the spread of white
settlements along America's ever-expanding western frontier.

By bribing mixed blood leader Levi Colbert and his brothers, who had by
now pretty well taken over the management of tribal affairs, Jackson and
Shelby secured a treaty on October 19, 1818, which extinguished the Chickasaw claim to the tribe's remaining land in both Tennessee and Kentucky. This
so-called Jackson Purchase was the largest single land cession by Indian
people within the present limits of Tennessee. It consisted of 10,700 square
miles or an area equal to about one-fourth of the entire state. Shortly before
concluding the negotiations, Jackson and Shelby, in order to protect the lives
of the Indian signers, agreed not to make public the official journal of the
treaty proceedings. Not until 1930, when Samuel Cole Williams published his
Beginnings of West Tennessee: In the Land of the Chickasaws, 1541–1841,
did the journal appear in print.

Within a few months after the cession of this vast tract of land, the town of
Memphis was laid out at the Lower Chickasaw Bluffs. Chickasaws continued
to frequent the Bluffs to trade for goods. Now, however, they were merely
visitors to an area that had once been theirs. Chickasaw hunting grounds had
been so drastically reduced by treaties that by 1819 their hunters were in a
pitiful condition. Whereas they had traditionally left small game for their
children to hunt, Chickasaw men were now bringing in geese and turkeys to
trade. Some hunters, in violation of the 1818 treaty, even wandered as far
north as present-day Weakley County in search of game from which skins
could be taken for use in bartering with the white traders. The hunters brought
their animal pelts to the Bluffs where they purchased ''well-watered'' whis-
key from unscrupulous peddlers and played their ball game on the level bluff
below Beale Street and in Fort Pickering. For over ten years after the Jackson
Purchase, the Chickasaws continued to trade their furs and skins for the wares
of the white traders at Memphis.

Andrew Jackson's elevation to the presidency in March 1829 foreshad-
owed the removal of the Chickasaws from their remaining lands in Missis-

---

(*Above*): Secretary of War Eaton warned the Chickasaws that the only alterna-
tive to removal to the trans-Mississippi West was submission to the laws of the
states in which they lived and disruption of tribal life. Courtesy of Library of
Congress. (*Below*): Cherokee Indian embassy, 1730, from the engraving by
Isaac Basire (see page 58). Courtesy of South Caroliniana Library, University
of South Carolina.

sippi and Alabama. Following the passage of Jackson's Indian Removal Bill by Congress in May 1830, Secretary of War John H. Eaton, a Tennessean and Old Hickory's former campaign manager, urged the Chickasaws and other southern Indians to meet with him to discuss their future. President Jackson left his duties at the White House in the summer of 1830 so that he could personally address the representatives of these tribes at a meeting at the Masonic Hall in Franklin, Tennessee. Only the Chickasaws attended the parley. Frustrated by the ongoing efforts of state officials in Mississippi and Alabama to destroy their tribal government, the Chickasaws signed a provisional agreement to emigrate to lands west of the Mississippi River at such time that the United States could provide them with "a country suitable to their wants and condition."

Although white settlers in Mississippi and Alabama drank numerous toasts to the signing of the treaty, no immediate removal ensued; Chickasaw leaders, taking full advantage of the provisional nature of the agreement, postponed their removal until 1837, when they finally worked out an arrangement to purchase lands in the West from the Choctaws. In the meantime, while negotiations with the Choctaws progressed, the Chickasaws made a determined effort to regain control of the Lower Chickasaw Bluffs from Tennessee by claiming that the southern border of the state had been incorrectly surveyed. Continuing pressure from white settlers, speculators, and government officials, however, finally forced tribal leaders to capitulate. They reluctantly agreed to relocate their people in what is today Oklahoma. The trek to the distant new homeland began in the summer of 1837 when Superintendent of Removal Arthur M. M. Upshaw of Pulaski, Tennessee, started enrolling the Chickasaw people for emigration. Their journey to Oklahoma brought great misery and suffering to the Chickasaws, largely as a result of the poor planning of American officials and the callousness of the businessmen who provided them with food and supplies. By early 1838, most of these Indians had been displaced to the West. A minister who accompanied them from Memphis to their new land poignantly captured the pathos of their exodus:

> There was not a true Chickasaw who would not have considered it a privilege to suffer death in any form or endure torture in any degree if by such suffering he could rescue the land of his birth and his love from the grasp of the white man, and make it a sure possession of his tribe. But he knew resistance was folly. He bowed to the fiat of Destiny, and turned from the land dearer to his heart than life.

5. Early Cherokee-White Relations

More than a hundred years passed after de Soto's visit in 1540 before the Cherokees in East Tennessee came into sustained contact with white colonists. On July 15, 1673, James Needham and Gabriel Arthur of the Virginia colony arrived at a Cherokee settlement in East Tennessee to negotiate for the opening of a trade route between the Cherokee domain and Virginia. By this agreement, the Virginia colony hoped to facilitate the exportation of animal pelts, beeswax, and bear oil to England. Before the end of the 1600s, Virginia and Carolina traders began dealing with the natives on a regular basis. The resulting impact on the Cherokees was tremendous.

By the end of the eighteenth century, there were many apparent changes in Cherokee society. Exposure to European ways, for example, had led to the building of more comfortable homes—log cabins with several rooms replaced earlier one-room dwellings—and European trade goods came to be regarded as necessities rather than luxuries. (Such goods eventually reduced the number of native handicrafts and replaced some altogether.)

Furthermore, the development of trade relations with the Europeans turned hunting in the Indian country into a business rather than a form of subsistence, and the increased reliance on hunting intensified warfare between the tribes. As the Creeks withdrew to the south, the entire valley of East Tennessee lay open to Cherokee expansion after 1715. Uniting with the Chickasaws in that year, the Cherokees also attempted to eliminate additional competition by driving the Shawnees from the fertile Cumberland River Valley.

Other areas of Indian life were affected by European contact as well. The introduction of domesticated animals such as horses made life easier, as did the presence of Negro slaves who sometimes worked side by side in the fields with Indians. These blacks were largely war booty or runaways from the English colonies whom the natives had captured. A number of Cherokees quickly realized the value of Negro slaves as servants and field workers, and some Indians soon began buying and selling them. As the black slave force increased in size, especially in the latter part of the eighteenth century, the Cherokees were able to produce a surplus of agricultural goods for sale; at the same time, men had more time to spend on hunting for trade. Thus agriculture and trade developed side by side as important aspects of the Cherokee economy. In exchange for pelts and farm goods, the English provided the Indian people with various tools, blankets, assorted wares, and, among other things, rum.

As indicated earlier, European contact also significantly influenced the Cherokee governmental organization by encouraging a movement away from the political authority of the nearly autonomous village of ancient times. A continuing state of tension with their Creek neighbors and intermittent hostilities with the British led the Cherokees more and more to political centralization. Contributing to this shift was the European tendency to treat the actions of the different tribesmen of scattered Cherokee villages as though all of the villages constituted a single governmental entity. The Indian people in one community, for example, might have their cornfields burned by Europeans in retaliation for the murder of a trader by an Indian from another town. Astute Cherokee leaders came to realize that they had a common stake in the outcome of the relations of their kinsmen with the Europeans. At the same time, the English openly encouraged Cherokees friendly to them to assume leadership positions.

In 1730 Sir Alexander Cuming, an unofficial envoy of King George II, designated Moytoy, a local chief from Tellico in the Overhill Towns, as "emperor" of the Cherokees in return for Moytoy's recognition of "his Majesty King George's Sovereignty over them." In the spring of that year, Cuming took seven Indians and their interpreter to England, where they were wined and dined and treated as visiting dignitaries, and English officials took advantage of the occasion to conclude Articles of Friendship and Commerce with the delegation. The articles committed the Cherokees to trade exclusively with England, guaranteed that whites would be tried in English courts for offenses against the natives in their tribal domain, promised the Indians rewards for returning fugitive slaves to their English masters, and pledged Cherokee military assistance if England went to war with any foreign power in North America.

Once back in their own country, the seven Cherokee spokesmen never tired of recounting the details of their visit to anyone who would listen. For over

---

(*Above*): This eighteenth-century engraving depicts Cunne Shote, a warrior from the Overhill country. Courtesy of University of Georgia Libraries, Athens, De Reune Collection. (*Below*): An artist's depiction of Fort Loudoun. From Lewis and Kneberg, *Tribes That Slumber: Indians of the Tennessee Region*.

twenty years their stories about King George II's majesty and power helped to keep the tribe aligned with the English. The most ardent defender of the English was Oukanaekah, who soon after his return from England was elected to the office of "white" or peace chief and renamed Attakullakulla, "the Little Carpenter" (because, like a carpenter, he could make every joint and notch in a controversy fit smoothly). A short man, about thirty years of age, Attakullakulla was an impressive speaker. During the mid-1730s, he used his oratorical skills repeatedly in an effort to discourage the Cherokees from aligning themselves with the French.

Despite the impassioned rhetoric of Attakullakulla, however, the French did gain some Cherokee friends, primarily because of the growing anti-English sentiment among the Indians. Trade abuses by the English were a source of constant complaint. In addition, as smallpox spread devastation in the Cherokee country, the "red" or war chief, Oconostota, accused the English of bringing this disease to his people in the trade goods they sold. A tall, handsome warrior, Oconostota grew increasingly hostile toward the English when his own face remained scarred after his recuperation from smallpox. He therefore sought to align the tribe with the French.

During the ensuing period of internal and external strife, the warrior element, represented by Oconostota, gained ascendency. The prestige of the "white" leaders declined and general confidence in them was severely shaken when their medicine men, using their most powerful herbs and all the prescribed rituals, were unable to halt the deaths from smallpox. Additionally, although the "white" chiefs had gained an effective leader in the mid-1700s, when the cool-headed and patient Old Hop, of the Cherokee capital of Chota, emerged as the *de facto* chief of the tribe (rivaling Moytoy's son, who had inherited the title of "emperor"), the tide of white settlement moving ever westward brought increasing conflicts, which automatically involved the warrior element. Another factor dividing the Cherokees was represented by the followers of Christian Gottlieb Priber, an obscure European who had arrived at Great Tellico in the country of the Overhill Cherokees in 1736 with the avowed purpose of establishing a utopian government to be called "The Kingdom of Paradise." By capitalizing on the divided loyalties of the Cherokees, Priber sparked a nationalistic revival that gained considerable support before English colonial officials labeled him a dangerous French agent and ordered his arrest in 1739. Thus, the Cherokees reacted to the existence of these many factions—some following the English, some the French, some Priber, and still others following individual Indian leaders. Warriors increasingly assumed a dominant role in the council meetings, and by the 1760s the "red" chiefs had been granted coercive political authority over the scattered villages.

Although contact with the whites led to important changes in Cherokee culture and to alterations in their government, the Cherokees borrowed only on a selective basis from the English. They undoubtedly wished to interact with the foreigners enough to obtain desired trade goods, but they neither desired to merge with the English nor accept completely their way of life. Traditionalism remained a strong factor in Cherokee society. In spite of persistent efforts by Anglican missionaries of the Society for the Propagation of the Gospel, for example, the Indians remained steadfast in their own religious beliefs and refused to incorporate the alien ideas and values of the Anglican church. Many of these native people doubted the sincerity of the ministers who preached the Gospel to them, especially when the Indians encountered the widespread drunkenness, dishonesty, and lack of charity and kindness that seemed to characterize the white society just over the hills.

Up until the mid-1700s, the Cherokees were able to achieve a stand-off with the Europeans by frequently reminding them that Indian trade and military assistance were as valuable to the intruders as trade goods were to the Indians. By 1750, however, the balance of power shifted as the tremendous population increase in the seaboard colonies pushed thousands of land-hungry colonials westward through gaps in the Appalachian Mountains to search for new land for settlement. At the same time international rivalries escalated into the armed struggle of the French and Indian War.

At the beginning of the war in 1756, the Cherokees encouraged the English to erect Fort Loudoun near the confluence of the Little Tennessee and Tellico rivers within five miles of the Cherokee capital at Chota. The natives promoted establishment of the fort in order to protect the families of Overhill warriors who had joined the British in fighting their French enemies. This friendly relationship with the English gradually deteriorated, however, as the Cherokees grew angry at the arrogance of English officials, and the anger turned to enmity when a number of Cherokee warriors returning from participation in an English campaign against Shawnees of the Ohio River region were killed and scalped by white frontiersmen. In the early part of 1760, therefore, Cherokee warriors under the "red" chief Oconostota surrounded Fort Loudoun and began a total siege. By the second week of August, the hungry and weary garrison surrendered. The Cherokees killed a number of the soldiers and civilians and later burned the fort to the ground to prevent the English from using it against them. Nevertheless, the "white" chief Attakullakulla, a powerful leader ever since his trip to England with Sir Alexander Cuming, was able to arrange a settlement of differences with the English in 1761 after French aid failed to materialize, leaving the Indians dependent on English supplies. Several hundred Cherokees from all parts of the tribal domain died during the French and Indian War.

Richard Henderson negotiates the Treaty of Sycamore Shoals. By Bernie Andrews in *The Overmountain Men* by Pat Alderman. Courtesy of Overmountain Press, Johnson City, Tennessee.

Although the English government sought to preserve peace and trade with the Indians by its Proclamation of 1763 which prohibited white settlement and private purchase of Indian land west of the Appalachian divide, North Carolinians and Virginians continued to trespass on Cherokee land in northeastern Tennessee. In the early 1770s squatters on the Watauga River evaded the rule against private purchase of land from the Indians by persuading some of the Cherokees to sign a perpetual *lease* of part of their domain. John Stuart, the English superintendent of Indian affairs for the southern tribes, joined with some outraged chiefs in opposing the actions of the whites, but the Watauga settlers were not to be dislodged. The Cherokees had earlier received a similar setback in Middle Tennessee when the Chickasaws, who had previously helped them evict the Shawnees from that region, moved onto lands the Cherokees claimed; and the Cherokee effort to challenge this eastward movement of the Chickasaws had been soundly defeated. But even though the Chickasaws made inroads on the Cherokee domain in Middle Tennessee and the Wataugans grabbed land in the east, more land was to be lost by the Cherokees—because not all tribal leaders were ready to halt land cessions to the white frontiersmen if this meant giving up trade goods.

This Cherokee desire for trade goods was used to good advantage by Richard Henderson in obtaining a huge land cession for his Transylvania Company. The astute North Carolina district judge had been so encouraged by the success of the Wataugans that he determined to purchase a vast territory in Kentucky and the Tennessee country. At a great parley with the Cherokees at Sycamore Shoals on the Watauga River in March 1775, Henderson's Transylvania company traded goods worth 10,000 pounds for a magnificent region bounded on the north and east by the Ohio and the Kentucky rivers and on the south by the ridge dividing the waters of the Tennessee and the Cumberland rivers.

The cession was eloquently opposed at the Sycamore Shoals council meeting by Dragging Canoe, Attakullakulla's son. This tall, middle-aged leader cautioned his father and the other older chiefs that the land sale would pave the way for the ultimate extinction of their people. When his father, the "white" chief, and Oconostota, the "red" chief, refused to be swayed by his arguments, Dragging Canoe turned to Henderson and angrily warned that the settlement of the area he had purchased would be "Dark and Bloody."

Dragging Canoe refused to recognize the Sycamore Shoals cession and resolved to recover possession of the land. During the summer of 1776 as the

---

Sandstone sculpture of Dragging Canoe by B. R. Allison. Courtesy of Tennessee Department of Conservation.

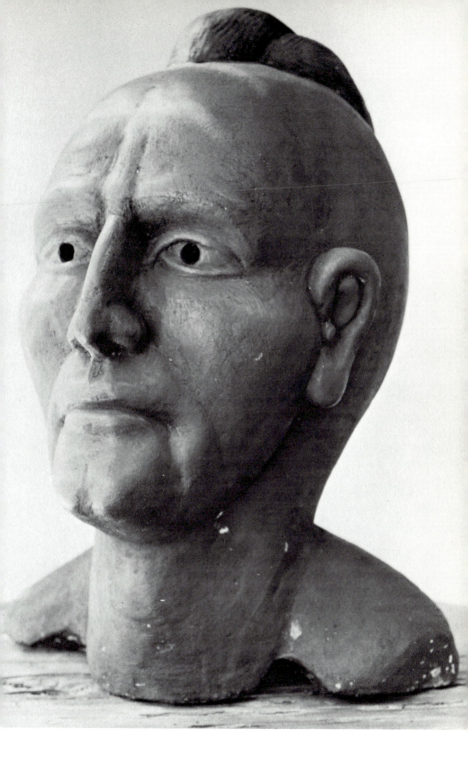

American colonies were declaring independence from their mother country, Cherokees sympathetic to Dragging Canoe's position showed their anger by carrying out a determined series of attacks against the white settlements in upper East Tennessee. In addition to resenting the colonials' insatiable appetite for land, the Cherokees had been stirred by rumors of an impending attack upon their towns by an American army of 6,000 men; so the Indians decided to strike first. When the time came for them to make a choice as the American Revolution reached the interior, they cast their lot with England.

Thus, while Thomas Jefferson's Declaration of Independence was catching the public's attention in the capitals throughout Europe, riflemen in East Tennessee, led by such noted fighters as James Robertson and John Sevier, were defending the American settlements against the Cherokee attacks. Fearing possible destruction of these settlements, a force of nearly 2,000 Wataugans, North Carolinians, and Virginians prepared in late September 1776 to invade the Overhill country. Completely overawed by the superior show of force by the Americans, the Cherokees abandoned their towns. The older chiefs agreed to make peace and to negotiage a new boundary line. Dragging Canoe was unwilling to be a party to the compact and withdrew from the Overhill Towns in the spring of 1777 as the treaty-making progressed. He led a large contingent of warriors and their families southwest to a location on Chickamauga Creek, where he established a new settlement near today's Chattanooga. Encouraged by the British, these Chickamaugans, as they were called, became the most hostile of all Cherokee warriors against the Americans in the Revolutionary War. Cherokee military action, however, was restricted largely to hit-and-run raids by small war parties. On the whole, the Overhill Indians tried hard to maintain peace and neutrality during the war.

Nevertheless, when the fortunes of war turned temporarily in favor of the English in 1779–1780, the Overhill Cherokees considered launching a concerted attack against the Americans. The involvement of the frontier settlers in the King's Mountain campaign in the northwestern corner of South Carolina seemed to offer a good opportunity for the Cherokees to recover their lost lands in upper East Tennessee. Unfortunately for them, Colonel John Sevier, fresh from victory at King's Mountain, led a force of North Carolinian-Wataugan riflemen toward the Overhill Towns at the same time that the Virginia militia under Colonel Arthur Campbell was making its way toward these Cherokee settlements. In December 1780 and January 1781 the Ameri-

Colonel John Sevier led an attack on the Overhill towns in the winter of 1780–81. Courtesy of Tennessee Historical Society.

cans ravaged or burned nearly every Overhill town. Following this crushing defeat, white settlers swarmed into the upper East Tennessee country.

In Middle Tennessee in 1779 and 1780, white settlement of the Cumberland River Valley only intensified Dragging Canoe's hatred of the Americans. He hoped first to isolate and obliterate the Middle Tennessee settlements and then to turn his attention to the East Tennessee intruders. With the aid of Creek and Shawnee allies who had come to Chickamauga Creek to join his force of Cherokee warriors, Dragging Canoe began his raids against the white settlements in the Cumberland Valley. At the same time, the Chickasaws, striking back against the American invasion of their hunting grounds, independently attacked these settlements as well.

The plight of the Cumberland pioneers became so desperate that James Robertson proposed an alliance with the Chickasaws to help discourage the other Indians from harassing the Cumberland area. John Sevier led an expedition against the Chickamaugans and other Cherokee warriors in the fall of 1782. Because the preliminary Treaty of Paris, which signaled the end of the American Revolutionary War, was signed on November 30, 1782, Sevier's raids against these Indians may be considered the last campaign of the war. Although open conflict between the Cherokees and the United States government officially ended two years after the Revolutionary War with the signing of the Treaty of Hopewell on November 28, 1785, Dragging Canoe continued his raids on white settlements in the Tennessee region.

Leaders in the American Congress had believed that the Treaty of Hopewell would establish peace and friendship between their new government and the Cherokees. The Cherokees, however, felt betrayed. They had conceded American ownership of a tract of land south of the Cumberland River in Tennessee and Kentucky, with the understanding that the rest of their domain would be closed to white settlement. Yet the frontiersmen were already violating the boundaries established by the treaty, and American officials had taken no action against the flagrant violations of these borders. When the government of the new nation was formed in 1789, President George Washington and other leaders sought to safeguard white squatters on Cherokee lands, while at the same time restoring the Indian tribe's confidence in the new nation. President Washington hoped to accomplish these seemingly incompatible goals by sending William Blount to persuade the Cherokees to cede tribal land southeast of the Clinch River, straddling what is today the Tennessee-North Carolina border, in exchange for a "solemn" guarantee of the Cherokees' right to all unceded lands. In the Treaty of Holston concluded on July 2, 1791, at what is now Knoxville, Blount even went so far as to empower the Cherokees to punish any Americans settling on their lands. The treaty also provided the Indians with an annuity of $1,000 (subsequently enlarged to $1,500) and promised to provide them with "useful implements of husbandry" and to help them to become "herdsmen and cultivators." Such gifts did not come cheaply to the natives. In addition to ceding tribal land to the Americans, the Cherokees had to allow "free and unmolested use of a road" between East Tennessee and the Cumberland settlements and grant the settlers the right to navigate the Tennessee River.

Not all Cherokees supported the treaties of Hopewell and Holston. From their Chickamaugan retreat, Dragging Canoe and his warriors, together with some of their kinsmen in their old haunts in East Tennessee, continued to struggle against the onrushing frontiersmen. By 1792 the so-called Five Lower Chickamaugan Towns of Running Water, Nickajack, Long Island, Crowtown, and Lookout Mountain Town contained an assorted group of hostile Cherokees, Shawnees, Creeks, and even white Tories. The towns especially attracted young, militant Indian warriors who sought a means of resisting the greed of the Americans and the diminishing tribal land base. In addition to staging raids against the growing white communities in the Cumberland River Valley area, these Chickamaugans sent an expedition against Knoxville in 1793.

The success of the Chickamaugans was limited. Their warriors were usually outnumbered, and few reinforcements were available; raiding parties were strictly voluntary; and a lack of unified command and a constant shortage of weapons and supplies further hampered their effort. The totality of the problems proved insurmountable. Despite inflicting heavy casualties on the whites, the Chickamaugans could not win.

In September 1794, a force of about 600 volunteers, including Cumberland settlers, marched under the command of Major James Ore toward the towns of Nickajack and Running Water and destroyed them. This expedition, coupled with the fact that Spanish support and northern Indian aid had been withdrawn, brought an end to the long struggle of the Chickamaugans. Deprived of the leadership of Dragging Canoe, who had died in 1792, and demoralized by the destruction of two of their towns, Chickamaugan resistance collapsed. The Indian leaders notified Territorial Governor William Blount that they were ready to make peace with the whites, and in November 1794 the splinter Chickamaugan group returned to the Cherokee tribe.

Following this reuniting of the Chickamaugans with the Cherokees, the United States government sought to exert its influence over the tribe in 1795 by establishing a "trading factory" at the Tellico Blockhouse on the Little Tennessee River near the original Fort Loudoun site. This trading post, together with the permanent Indian agency set up in the Tennessee region six years later, was designed to have "a very salutary effect upon the minds of the Indians." American traders—or the goods they dispensed—did indeed have

CUMBERLAND MOUNTAINS

Sequatchie River

TO WALTON ROAD

WALDEN RIDGE

TO CUMBERLAND GAP

TO NASHVILLE

Battle Creek

○ Tuskegee

Chick

○ Citico

Chattanoo

GREAT WAR TRAIL

TENN.

① Running Water

② Nickajack

④ Lookout Mountain Town

ALA.

③ Long Island

GA.

TENNESSEE RIVER

⑤

Crowtown

SAND MOUNTAIN

TO WILLSTOWN AND PENSACOLA

LOOKOUT MOUNTAIN

0   10

SCALE OF MILES

○ Willstown

an impact on the Indians, but not in the long run a salutary one. Although more than forty years were to pass before the actual removal of these native people, trade goods and white pressures, among other factors, were setting an irreversible pattern—one that would lead to the eventual eviction of all but a small remnant of the Cherokees from their beloved homeland.

The Five Lower Towns. From Raulston and Livingood, *Sequatchie: A Story of the Southern Cumberlands*.

6. The Cherokees and "The White Man's Road"

When Tennessee entered the Union in 1796, the Cherokees and the Chicka-saws claimed about three-fourths of the state's territory. By 1818 the Chicka-saws had given up their title to land in Tennessee, and by 1835 all Cherokee claims in the state had been extinguished by the United States; only a few more years were necessary to effect the actual removal of the Cherokees. The history of the Cherokees between 1796 and the time of their ultimate departure from Tennessee is the story of a remarkable effort to hold on to their land by accepting "the white man's road." That history is also the story of a Trail of Tears leading from Tennessee and neighboring southern states to present-day Oklahoma.

Unhappy with American recognition of Cherokee boundaries in the 1791 Treaty of Holston, white North Carolinians argued that the Indians had forfeited their title to land in the Tennessee country because of their wartime alliance with the British. American settlers, disregarding boundaries estab-lished by the treaty, streamed into the area. In 1797 when President John Adams sent United States troops to expel intruders from Cherokee lands, the Tennessee legislature objected to such an act of "violent oppression" against its citizens. Thereupon the Treaty of Tellico was signed in 1798, the first of a series of treaties that further whittled down Cherokee holdings in Tennessee and elsewhere in the South.

In 1801 the Tennessee legislature enlarged the boundaries of several of its counties so as to include within them all lands claimed by the Cherokees. François André Michaux, a Frenchman traveling through the Cherokee coun-try in Tennessee in 1802, noted that the "illiberal proceedings" of American frontiersmen were responsible for inflaming the Indians; according to Mi-chaux, white settlers deliberately incited conflicts with the natives in order to have excuses for seizing their land. In addition, the French visitor claimed that, contrary to statements by white Tennesseans, it was the Cherokees who needed military protection by the United States Army, not the white fron-tiersmen. The administration of Thomas Jefferson, however, responded to the demands of Tennesseans for more Indian land by using bribery to negotiate land cession treaties. This technique was used to secure the Third Treaty of Tellico in 1805 (the Second Treaty of Tellico did not include any land in Tennessee) and the treaty negotiated in Washington in 1806 by Secretary of War Henry Dearborn. Then, in 1817, in spite of Cherokee assistance against the Creek Red Sticks during the War of 1812, President James Monroe responded to growing pressure from white Tennesseans by sending two of them—Governor Joseph McMinn and General Andrew Jackson—together with General David Meriwether of Georgia to negotiate a removal treaty with the Cherokees. In the treaty they obtained, and in a subsequent one secured in 1819 by Secretary of War John C. Calhoun, the United States restricted Cherokee holdings in Tennessee to the southeastern corner of the state.

By 1820 the Cherokee country in Tennessee and elsewhere in the South had become an island in an engulfing sea of white settlements. The Cherokees, numbering less than 14,000 natives that year, were surrounded by a white population of greater numbers. Because of their continual loss of land in the southern Appalachian country, the Cherokees moved many of their towns from Tennessee, most from North Carolina, and all from South Carolina to Georgia, where they established a new capital. There was, however, no escape from the white man. Many tribal leaders had realized long ago that the imbalance in military power between the Indians and their white neighbors made any thought of armed resistance in their homeland against the Americans preposterous.

Some Cherokees sought isolation from white society by moving to present-day western Arkansas. Encouraged by United States officials to settle there, several thousand Indians, including many from Tennessee, migrated westward in the late 1820s and joined others who had earlier sought refuge there. (It was among these Cherokees that Sam Houston found the solitude he sought after resigning the governorship of Tennessee in 1829.) Although the Cherokees West, as they were called, urged their eastern kinsmen to join them in their new homeland, many influential Cherokee statesmen chose a different course for dealing with the pressures from the whites.

Between 1820 and the early 1830s these leaders sought American recognition of Cherokee independence, tribal integrity, and land boundaries by demonstrating their ability to travel down ''the white man's road.'' Behind this effort to adopt American patterns of living were two important groups—the mixed bloods, whose white parents had already served as an opening wedge for pervasive changes in tribal society, and the Christian missionaries, who were now receiving a warmer welcome among the Cherokees (especially from the mixed bloods) and who brought the Indians not only the religion of the dominant white society, but also its pattern of family life and economic division of labor.

The Cherokees had already made several advances toward this end. Indeed
the Christian missionaries whose religious revivals swept the American
frontier during the early 1800s had won many Indian converts. Men like
Gideon Blackburn, whose Presbyterian parish in Maryville, Tennessee, bordered the Cherokee country, led such "Christianizing" efforts among the
natives. The Cherokees, however, were generally much more interested in the
secular education offered by most missionaries than in their evangelizing.
Blackburn, for example, in 1804 opened his first school for Cherokee youth
on the Hiwassee River in the Overhill country near the present town of
Charleston, Tennessee; a year later Tennessee Governor John Sevier, who
had commanded troops in thirty-five recorded battles against the Cherokees,
openly shed tears of joy at the sight of Indian children, dressed in white man's
clothing, reading aloud from English books at Blackburn's school. In 1816
the Congregationalist minister Cyrus Kingsbury established Brainerd Mission
with a boarding school for Indians near present-day Chattanooga. Other
missionaries started schools too, receiving encouragement from the Cherokees as well as from the federal government and Tennessean Andrew Jackson,
who in spite of his relentless efforts to push the Indians westward nevertheless
exhibited warm regard for many of them as individuals.

Some Indians embraced education with an excited fervor, and English soon
became a second language for many of them. Meanwhile in 1821, Sequoyah,
a middle-aged Cherokee of mixed blood who was born in the village of
Tuskegee in present-day Monroe County, Tennessee, astounded his people
by showing them how they could read and write in their own language. For
years this lame silversmith and artist had been fascinated by the "talking
leaves" (printed pages) of the Americans, even though he could not read or
write English. Since the early 1800s, white missionaries in the Tennessee
country had tried unsuccessfully to transcribe the Cherokee language into
written form. Around 1809, Sequoyah became obsessed with the idea of
creating a writing system for the Cherokees, and he continued to work steadily
at the task after his departure in 1818 to live with the Cherokees West in
Arkansas. Eventually he devised an alphabet of eighty-six characters (one
character was later discarded) using various English, Greek, and Hebrew

---

(*Above*): This Lloyd Branson painting shows the blockhouse fort built in
Knoxville in 1793 to protect the territorial capital from Indian attack. Cour-
tesy of *Knoxville News-Sentinel* (see page 69). (*Below*): Sequoyah, the
Cherokee Cadmus, as depicted by Charles Bird King in 1828. From Bureau of
American Ethnology *Nineteenth Annual Report*, courtesy Special Collec-
tions, University of Tennessee Library, Knoxville.

letters (unable to read the characters, he placed some of them upside down and sideways) to represent each of the Cherokee syllables. Then in 1821, he returned east to demonstrate his syllabary to skeptical tribal leaders by writing a message which his young daughter read and answered. Astonished and impressed by the demonstration, tribal leaders officially approved the syllabary.

In 1822 Sequoyah returned to Arkansas to teach his writing system to the Cherokees West. Six years later he went to Washington as their special envoy and was one of the signers of a treaty that exchanged the Cherokee land in Arkansas for an extensive tract in what is now northeastern Oklahoma. Sequoyah's syllabary enabled the Cherokees in the East and those in the West to communicate more easily.

Sequoyah's invention, together with the adoption of English as a second language by the tribe, led to remarkable advances in literacy among the Cherokees. Within a few years after Sequoyah produced his syllabary, many Cherokees could read and write in their own language. According to a Moravian missionary, "the whole [Cherokee] nation became an academy for the study of the [new writing] system." Samuel A. Worcester, another missionary who had arrived at Brainerd Mission in 1825, reported to his superiors in New England that:

> Young Cherokees travel a great distance to be instructed in this easy method of writing and reading. In three days they are able to commence letter-writing and return home to their villages prepared to teach others. It is the opinion of some of the missionaries that if the Bible were translated and printed according to the plan here described, hundreds of adult Cherokees who will never learn English, would be able to read it in a single month.

Before the end of 1825, a Cherokee translation of the New Testament was available. Then, in January 1828, Worcester played an instrumental role in securing a printing press with Sequoyan type for the Cherokees.

Reading soon emerged as a favorite pastime among a number of those Indians wealthy enough to own books and to subscribe to periodicals. On February 21, 1828, the Cherokees began publishing their own newspaper, the *Cherokee Phoenix*, under the editorship of Elias Boudinot, a young mixed blood who had previously attended an American school at Cornwall, Connecticut, and had married a white girl. Boudinot published the newspaper in a bilingual format that carried items in Cherokee and English in parallel col-

---

The Cherokee syllabary invented by Sequoyah. From Bureau of American Ethnology *Nineteenth Annual Report*, courtesy Special Collections, University of Tennessee Library, Knoxville.

Cherokee Alphabet.

Ꭰ a	Ꭱ e	Ꭲ i	Ꭳ o	Ꭴ u	Ꭵ v
Ꭶ ga Ꭷ ka	Ꭸ ge	Ꭹ gi	Ꭺ go	Ꭻ gu	Ꭼ gv
Ꭽ ha	Ꭾ he	Ꭿ hi	Ꮀ ho	Ꮁ hu	Ꮂ hv
Ꮃ la	Ꮄ le	Ꮅ li	Ꮆ lo	Ꮇ lu	Ꮈ lv
Ꮉ ma	Ꮊ me	Ꮋ mi	Ꮌ mo	Ꮍ mu	
Ꮎ na Ꮏ hna Ꮐ nah	Ꮑ ne	Ꮒ ni	Ꮓ no	Ꮔ nu	Ꮕ nv
Ꮖ qua	Ꮗ que	Ꮘ qui	Ꮙ quo	Ꮚ quu	Ꮛ quv
Ꮜ sa Ꮝ s	Ꮞ se	Ꮟ si	Ꮠ so	Ꮡ su	Ꮢ sv
Ꮣ da Ꮤ ta	Ꮥ de Ꮦ te	Ꮧ di Ꮨ ti	Ꮩ do	Ꮪ du	Ꮫ dv
Ꮬ dla Ꮭ tla	Ꮮ tle	Ꮯ tli	Ꮰ tlo	Ꮱ tlu	Ꮲ tlv
Ꮳ tsa	Ꮴ tse	Ꮵ tsi	Ꮶ tso	Ꮷ tsu	Ꮸ tsv
Ꮹ wa	Ꮺ we	Ꮻ wi	Ꮼ wo	Ꮽ wu	Ꮾ wv
Ꮿ ya	Ᏸ ye	Ᏹ yi	Ᏺ yo	Ᏻ yu	Ᏼ yv

Sounds represented by Vowels.

a, as a in father, or short as a in rival
e, as a in hate, or short as e in met
i, as i in pique, or short as i in pit

o, as aw in law, or short as o in not
u, as oo in fool, or short as u in pull
v, as u in but, nasalized

Consonant Sounds

… nearly as in English, but approaching to k. d nearly as in English but approaching … h k l m n q s t w y as in English. Syllables beginning with g except Ꭶ have sometimes the … er of k. Ꭺ Ꮝ Ꮩ are sometimes sounded to, tu, tv and Syllables written with tl except Ꮭ sometimes vary to dl.

umns. Early issues of the publication were printed on paper manufactured in Knoxville and hauled by wagon to the press in Georgia. The *Phoenix* was sold in many states in order to familiarize the American public with the progress of the tribe. American readers were especially pleased by articles in the newspaper which demonstrated that the Cherokees were adopting various aspects of white culture.

One sign of Cherokee acceptance of the ways of the white man appeared in the manner in which the Indians built their houses. Although the Cherokees had long constructed their dwellings out of logs, they usually now split and fit the lumber together by notching, as was the custom of white builders on the southern frontier. Typical Cherokee houses ranged from fifteen to twenty-five feet square and were divided into separate rooms. These cabins, had wooden, unfinished floors and roofs of split-oak shingles. Each dwelling was heated by an open fireplace, which also provided light and a place for cooking; the smoke from the fireplace escaped through a wooden chimney made of sticks and short logs chinked together with clay and mud. Some cabins had lofts and porches, but very few had windows.

While most Cherokees lived in homes similar to the ones of ordinary white frontiersmen, the more affluent Indians, especially the mixed bloods, built houses that rivaled those of even upperclass whites. By 1835 Joseph Vann, a mixed blood known as ''Rich Joe'' to his fellow tribesmen, owned extensive property in Tennessee's Hamilton County, including 35 assorted buildings, 110 slaves, a mill, a ferry, and 300 acres of fertile land on which he raised about 3,200 bushels of corn. Vann's property offers just one indication of the rising prosperity, measured in American terms, of the Cherokees. By the mid-1830s, according to a tribal census taken by the United States, they had more than 8,000 houses of various types for their 2,637 families. Very few Cherokees even approached being as well off as Vann, however. George Featherstonhaugh, an English traveler who journeyed through the Tennessee River country at that time, reported that Indians at the lower level of society lived in floorless, ''rude'' log cabins, the poorest people among them suffering a wretched existence.

After 1800 an increasingly large number of Cherokees had followed the advice of President Thomas Jefferson and his successors in the White House by returning to agriculture as a basic means of support. Although traditionally the Cherokees had been agriculturalists, the deerskin trade had changed their

---

The *Cherokee Phoenix* began publication on February 21, 1828, in the bilingual format that appears here. Courtesy Special Collections, University of Tennessee Library, Knoxville.

PROTECTION

ᏣᎳᎩ ᏧᎴᏫᏍᏓᏁᎯ.
CHEROKEE PHŒNIX.

OL. I. NEW ECHOTA, WEDNESDAY MAY 14, 1828. NO. 12.

BY ELIAS BOUDINOTT
RINTED WEEKLY BY
ACH. HARRIS,
THE CHEROKEE NATION.

if paid in advance, $3 in six
$3 50 if paid at the end of the

cribers who can read only the
anguage the price will be $2,00
or $2,50 to be paid within the

bscription will be considered as
unless subscribers give notice to
y before the commencement of a

son procuring six subscribers,
ing responsible for the payment,
ve a seventh gratis.

ements will be inserted at seven-
ts per square for the first inser-
thirty-seven and a half cents for
nuance; longer ones in propor-

letters addressed to the Editor,
will receive due attention.

[illegible]

FOR THE CHEROKEE PHŒNIX.

wing persons are authorized to
criptions and payments for the
Phœnix.

Hill, Esq. Treasurer of the A.
, Boston, Mass.
M. Tracy, Agent of the A. B.
ew York.
D. Eddy, Canandaigua, N. Y.
& Converse, Richmond, Va.
es Campbell, Beaufort, S. C.
rge Smith, Statesville, W. T.
sney Roberts—Powal Me.
s. R. Gold, an itinerant Gen-

ROKEE LAWS.

[CONTINUED.]

Town Nov. 8. 1825.

d by the National Committee cil, That the law authoriz- pointment of light horse com- ssed at Brown's Town on day of September, 1808, be- me is hereby repealed, and u of light horse companies. sheriff, deputy sheriff and ables shall be chosen & ap- r each district, in the fol- nner; to wit: rshals to be elected by the Com. and the principal sher- elected by the people in their e districts; and the two con- by the people within their bounds, for the term of . The marshals and sher- enter into bond and give two ood and sufficient securities sum of not less than one thou- rs. The sheriffs to appoint deputies, and for whose con- shall also be held responsi- und. The constables shall bond and give two good se- the penal sum of two hun- rs. The duties of the mar- sheriffs shall be to make of all just debts, such as and, liquidated accounts and ts, & to arrest horse thieves rogues and murderers for rding to law. ies of the constables shall e as that of the marshals s, but they shall be confined ir respective bounds in ex- eir official duties; and each e named officers are here- zed, when in pursuit of crim- mmons as many men as may ry to arrest such criminals. rson or persons refusing to out any reasonable excuse, ons, he or they shall forfeit fine of twenty-five dollars such offence; to be recover- e same way and manner as ebts, and the fines so col- ll be paid into the national treasury. The person or persons o-beying such summons, upon presenting the officer's certificate before the national treasury, for the service so performed, shall be entitled to receive one dollar per day for the time so engaged from actual necessity. The constables, when executing their duties in arresting & conducting criminals to the place of trial, shall also be entitled to one dollar per day for the time actually engaged. Each marshal shall be entitled to receive forty dollars, and each principal sheriff shall be entitled to receive thirty dollars per annum for their services from the public funds, in addition to their fees of eight per cent. for collections. The deputy sheriffs and constables shall also be entitled to receive eight per cent. for collections.

By order,
JNO. ROSS, Pres't N. Com.
MAJOR RIDGE, Speaker.
his
Approved—PATH ⋈ KILLER.
mark.
A. M'COY, Clerk of N. Com.
E. BOUDINOTT, Clerk N. Council.

New Town, Nov. 9. 1825.

Resolved by the National Committee and Council, That all written wills, bearing the signature of the testator and signed by one or two respectable witnesses, and the same appearing to the satisfaction of the court of the district wherein the testator lived, or where most of his estate may be situated, that it is the last will & testament of the deceased such will and testament shall be valid and binding to all intents and purposes.

Be it further resolved, That nothing shall be construed in the foregoing, so as to impair or destroy the validity of any will having no witnesses, which may be found among the valuable papers of the deceased, bearing his or her signature, which will and signature, shall be satisfactorily proved to be the hand writing of the deceased.

Be it further resolved, That nuncupative wills, where witnesses are called, and the testator, in the presence of two or three respectable persons, at his or her last sickness, make known his or her will, and one of the witnesses being a disinterested person, such nuncupative wills being committed to writing in ten days after the testators decease, and the same appearing to the satisfaction of the district court to be agreeable to the testators last will and testament, such wills shall also be valid and binding.

Be it further resolved, That where a person possessing property and dies intestate, and having a wife and children, the property of the deceased, shall be equally divided among his lawful and acknowledged children, allowing the widow a share with the children, after all just debts of the deceased shall have been paid by those obtaining letters of administration, agreeably to law, and in case the deceased leave a wife without children, then in that case, the widow shall be entitled to receive one fourth of the estate, after said estate shall have been freed from incumbrance of all just and lawful demands, and the residue of the estate to go to his nearest kin; and in case a woman claiming and having exclusive right to property, dies and leaves a husband and children, her property shall revert to her children and husband, in the same manner as above stated and provided for.

By order of the National Com.
JNO ROSS, Pres't N. Com.
MAJOR RIDGE, Speaker.
his
PATH ⋈ KILLER.
mark.
CHARLES R. HICKS.
A. M'COY, Clerk N. Com.
E. BOUDINOTT, Clk. N. Council.

New Town, Nov. 10, 1825.

Resolved by the National Committee and Council, That any person or persons, whatsoever, who shall lay violent hands upon any female, by forcibly attempting to ravish her chastity contrary to her consent, abusing her person, and committing a rape upon such female, he or they, so offending, upon conviction before any of the district or circuit judges, for the first offence, shall be punished with fifty lashes upon the bare back and the left ear cropped off close to the head; for the second offence, one hundred lashes and the other ear cut off; for the third offence, death.

Be it further resolved, That any woman or women, making evidence against any man, and falsely accusing him of having laid violent hands upon any woman, with intent of committing a rape upon her person, and sufficient proof having been adduced in any of the district or circuit judges, to refute the testimony of such woman or women, she or they so offending, shall be punished with twenty-five stripes upon her or their bare back, to be inflicted by any of the marshals, sheriffs or constables.

By order,
JOHN ROSS, Pres't N. Com.
MAJOR RIDGE, Speaker.
his
Approved—PATH ⋈ KILLER.
mark.
CHARLES R. HICKS.
A. M'COY, Clerk N. Com.
E. BOUDINOTT, Clk. N. Coun.

New Town, Nov. 10, 1825.

Whereas, it has been represented to the general council, that much injury is sustained by the inhabitants living on the boundary lines, from citizens of the United States, feeding and keeping their stock of property on Cherokee lands, whereby horses, cattle, hogs &c. belonging to the citizens of this nation, are exposed to be taken off by such persons, trespassing; therefore.

Resolved by the National Committee and Council, That the circuit judges are hereby authorised and directed, to appoint an assistant ranger in their respective districts, which border on the boundary lines of the United States, whose residence shall be nearest to said boundary line, and whose duty it shall be, to put strict attention to such trespasses herein complained of, & to forward the frontier inhabitants of the United States in the adjoining counties, against placing, keeping and feeding their horses, cattle, hogs, sheep or goats on Cherokee lands; and to take up, post, and dispose of, all such property which may be found within their respective bounds, agreeably to the laws respecting estrays, and any citizen or citizens of the United States reclaiming and proving away any such property, and be unable to produce satisfactory proof, that he, she or they, did not wilfully place such property on Cherokee lands, to feed and graze thereon, the assistant ranger, in that case, is hereby authorised and required, to exact a fine of two dollars for every horse, gelding or mare, and one dollar for every head of black cattle, and twenty-five cents for every head of swine, sheep or goats, so proven away. Such fines shall be in addition to the fees allowed by law to the rangers for their posting, keeping and selling estrays; but in case sufficient proof can be adduced to shew that such property was not wilfully placed on Cherokee lands to feed or graze thereon, and that such property had merely strayed thereon unknown to the owner or owners; then in that case, the fine herein imposed, shall not be exacted; excepting the necessary expenses and fees allowed by law in such cases.

Be it further resolved, That the assistant ranger is hereby required to observe and pay strict attention to the same rules and regulations required of rangers by law, and who shall also be entitled to the same fees of eight per cent. on the amount collected for the fines herein imposed, the remainder for the benefit of the national treasury.

By order of the National Committee,
JNO. ROSS, Pres't N. Com.
MAJOR RIDGE, Speaker.
PATH ⋈ KILLER.
A. M'COY, Clerk, N. Com.
ELIJAH HICKS, Clerk N. Council.

[illegible]

TT ᏍᏊ, 8 ... 1825.

[illegible]

TT ᏍᏊ, 9 ... 1825.

[illegible]

TT ᏍᏊ, 10 ... 1825.

[illegible]

TT ᏍᏊ, 10 ... 1825.

[illegible]

way of living. Thus when the idea of emphasizing agriculture had been proposed in the Holston Treaty of 1791, it was not enthusiastically adopted by the Indians at that time. Ten years later, however, with Cherokee lands diminishing rapidly and the remaining holdings more and more traversed by American roads, the readoption of agriculture became as much a necessity as an effort to emulate American ways. By the 1830s the natives had made such progress in this endeavor that a Cherokee Indian family without a farm was the exception rather than the rule. The Indians extended their settlements away from their old town centers and began operating their farms on an individual basis, although the land itself remained communal property. The resulting population pattern resembled that of their white neighbors in the plantation South.

By 1835 the Cherokee families in the South had over 3,000 farms with some 44,000 acres of land under cultivation. In Tennessee alone, according to incomplete census figures, there were 412 Cherokee farms with nearly 10,700 acres under cultivation producing about 130,000 bushels of corn and 1,000 bushels of wheat. The estimated worth of the tillable Cherokee land in Tennessee, figured at two dollars an acre, was $443,290. The entire Cherokee domain in the South, over 20,000 square miles, was larger than Massachusetts, Connecticut, and Rhode Island combined and contained tillable land valued at more than 2.4 million dollars.

Since the early 1800s livestock production had also experienced a steady growth, especially the raising of swine and cattle in the Tennessee area. Part of the credit for the advances in dairying among the Cherokees must go to Nancy Ward, a "Beloved Woman" who was a niece of Attakullakulla. Ward had learned how to make butter and cheese in 1776 while sheltering the wife of William Bean, Tennessee's first permanent white settler, from Cherokee warriors, and she soon bought cattle in order to introduce dairying to her people. As will be noted later, Cherokee progress in livestock production and dairying, as well as in agriculture, was partly the result of black slave labor.

Other pursuits also proved to be highly profitable for the Indians. Sawmills and gristmills became fairly common and a thriving commerce took shape. As whites developed roads through their domain, the Cherokees established "stands" or public accommodations at strategic spots, set up tollgates, and maintained turnpikes. In 1817 the United States Post Office began service in the Cherokee region by locating the first office at Ross's Landing near the foot of Market Street in present-day Chattanooga. The Cherokees also operated ferries on the rivers.

Cherokee clothing and accessories in the 1800s also changed. Upperclass Indians, particularly the mixed bloods, adopted the garb of the American citizens. The spread of cotton culture on Indian lands and the introduction of the spinning wheel and the weaving paraphernalia of the Americans facilitated the manufacture of cloth and clothing by native women. Leaders such as mixed blood John Ross and full blood Major Ridge dressed like refined gentlemen of the Old South. As time went by, trousers of buckskin or cloth often replaced the traditional leggings for men, although many Indians continued to wear the hip-length shirt made of buckskin, calico, or home-woven material. Some of the men also followed the practice of wearing earrings, slitting their ears to accommodate such adornments; some wore hats while others wore turbans made from calico; and some wore white man's shoes, while many Indians still preferred the traditional moccasins.

Even Cherokee diet showed the growing influence of the living patterns of the whites. Corn and beans remained the staple foods for a majority of the people, but white contact helped to bring about rise in the quality and variety of food for the upperclass groups.

One negative aspect of emulating the whites, however, proved very troublesome to the Cherokees. The excessive consumption of liquor, especially among more affluent Cherokees, was a serious problem that native leaders made little progress in curbing. Associated with the drinking bouts of some Cherokees was their great pastime, the ball game. Christian missionaries viewed the game as "backsliding" because drinking and heavy gambling frequently accompanied it.

In addition to the ball game, other ancient tribal sports and traditional forms of recreation were also perpetuated by the Cherokees as they followed an increasingly bicultural existence. Especially popular was the sport of "stalk-shooting," a game that made use of their skill at archery. Dancing served as a form of recreation and, as in the case of the Green Corn Dance which they still observed, a link to traditionalism. "Dancing frolics," as the missionaries called them, were common among those Cherokees least willing to accept American habits.

Thus the Cherokees adopted many aspects of the white culture, but a marked tendency to cling to older customs existed in some areas. While the natives utilized the white man's medical cures, for example, they continued to have deep respect for ancient practices and tribal medicine men. A case in point was their attempt to combat the smallpox and consumption that plagued the tribe after the turn of the century. Although they called upon white doctors for help, the Indians also relied on more traditional means of ridding themselves of the "evil" that afflicted them. During one epidemic in 1824, as smallpox reached within twenty miles of Calhoun, Tennessee, a missionary reported that "the Old Conjuror has appointed a great Phy[sic] dance . . . promising that all who join him, shall not be afflicted with the disease." Cherokees also sought the help of medicine men when preparing for their ball games, as they once had done when preparing for war.

Another area where ancient customs persisted was in the realm of marriage. At one time the Cherokees apparently had very little regard for the white man's cherished principle of the sanctity of marriage to one wife; under the influence of missionaries, however, the natives began to pass laws against having multiple mates. And although some polygamy continued to exist, more and more Indians were married in Christian services. By the late 1820s, the *Cherokee Phoenix* was publishing social notes with detailed descriptions of the beautiful white cambric gowns of Indian brides and the "clean northern domestic" suits of their grooms. Reminiscent of the older deference to women, on the other hand, was the continuing practice of allowing a widow to drop the name of her deceased husband in order to resume her maiden name.

Despite the tendency to cling to some older customs and modes of behavior, the Cherokees were making steady advances along "the white man's road." This was especially true in the political realm, as the natives sought to strengthen their government and society in order to maintain their sovereignty over an ever-shrinking tribal domain. The weaknesses of Cherokee tribal government described earlier continued to plague the Indians in the early 1800s. Although delegates from various towns met periodically as a tribal body called the National Council, the implementation of a unified tribal policy on any given matter was hampered by the lack of any mechanism other than informal social pressure to force compliance. Some progress was made along these lines in 1808 when the National Council adopted a written legal code in English and ordered the establishment of tribal "regulating parties" to "suppress horse stealing and robbery of other property." Two years later the council again sought to promote tribal unity by canceling all outstanding blood debts between the clans. Then, in response to pressure from Andrew Jackson and other white Tennesseans for land cessions following the Red Stick War, the Cherokees adopted another measure to strengthen their government. Seeking a way to permit the tribe to reach a unified position on various issues more quickly, the council in 1817 established a thirteen member "Standing Committee"—later referred to as the National Committee—to supervise tribal affairs subject to the review and unanious consent of the National Council. Yet even this innovation failed to protect the Cherokees

John Ross, principal chief of the Cherokees from 1828 until his death in 1866. Courtesy of Bureau of American Ethnology Collection, National Anthropological Archives, Smithsonian Institution.

from the appetite of Americans for Indian land. Two years later, Calhoun's Treaty of 1819 stripped them of more than half of their remaining domain in Tennessee and North Carolina.

Following this land cession, the Cherokees firmly resolved to resist future treaty-making overtures by the United States. Many Cherokee political leaders had come to realize that, despite the recent trend toward greater centralization of power, their lack of political discipline was responsible for their continuing loss of tribal territory to the whites. Individual freedom of decision and action had long been an accepted social pattern among their people, but the leaders recognized that such indulgences could no longer be allowed. Only organized and authoritative responses, they insisted, could cope with the threats imposed by the white man. In 1820 these Indian leaders restructured their government to ensure wider participation in tribal affairs and to provide closer supervision of relations with the Americans. They also established a police power—the "lighthorse"—to compel their citizens' obedience to tribal laws and to regulate their behavior. The strongest influence behind these and subsequent changes along similar lines were men educated in white schools and acquainted with the workings of the American government and society.

The guiding hand of these new leaders was John Ross, the son of a Scottish trader who had lived among the Cherokees for years, and of a mother who was one-fourth Cherokee. Born near present-day Center, Alabama, in 1790, Ross moved with his parents to several locations within the Cherokee country before his father settled near the foot of Lookout Mountain on Chattanooga Creek. As a lad, Ross was educated at home by a white tutor and then by white teachers at Reverend Gideon Blackburn's mission school and at the Kingston Academy. Although he was only one-eighth Cherokee, spoke the native language haltingly at best, and never learned Sequoyah's syllabary, Ross early identified himself with the Cherokees and developed a firm attachment to the concept of tribal unity on the ancestral domain. Ross made many friends among the full bloods. Since he was fluent in English and was an able orator, they considered him a valuable asset in their dealings with the Americans. During the early 1800s Ross served as an aide and confidant to tribal leaders. He came to be regarded by many Indians, according to one observer, as "the hope of the [Cherokee] Nation."

At the age of twenty-three, Ross was an adjutant in a mounted Cherokee regiment that served with Andrew Jackson's forces against the Creek Red Sticks. Later, he became president of the newly created National Committee, and he put aside his business activities at Ross's Landing to devote maximum time to the development of the Cherokee national government and to the defense of the tribal domain against white incursions. Ross's efforts culmi-

nated on July 26, 1827, in the adoption of a written constitution by the
Cherokees. Modeled after the American Constitution, the document boldly
proclaimed the existence of an independent Cherokee Nation with complete
sovereignty over its land in Tennessee, North Carolina, Alabama, and Georgia.

This constitution marked the first effort by Indians in North America to
establish a complete political structure providing for the self-government of
their people under written laws enacted entirely by democratic processes. The
Cherokees believed that this step proved once and for all their right to be
considered as an independent political unit and as a distinct ethnic enclave.
Some thought that territorial status under the American Constitution or
perhaps even admission as a separate state might be eventual possibilities. A
few leaders believed that the creation of the District of Columbia years earlier
by the United States on land ceded by Maryland and Virginia offered a
precedent by which their rights might be protected.

A group of full bloods, led by an Indian named, ironically, Whitepath, and
other traditionalists had fiercely objected to the new Constitution and the
adoption of Christianity and the white man's ways. Such deviations from
tribal laws and customs, they warned, would only lead to the further decay of
tribal integrity. The pleas of these traditionalists for a return to the old lifestyle
fell on deaf ears for the most part.

On the other hand Ross, who was elected principal chief in 1828, and his
followers, who constituted the growing majority, believed that success in
adopting American culture was the only way to maintain Cherokee sovereignty over their shrunken tribal domain. To that end, Ross had helped to
secure the passage of a constitutional provision excluding anyone who dis-
believed in the Christian God from holding office or giving testimony in a
court of law. And, in 1829, to be certain that the United States would not
obtain any additional land cessions, Major Ridge, who became an adviser to
Ross, helped to formalize the "Blood Law," making it an offense punishable
by death for anyone to relinquish any land without the consent of the "National Authorities." (Major Ridge himself was among those later executed for
this crime!) Ross and Ridge hoped that, as the *Cherokee Phoenix* once
editorialized, "the astonishing progress" of the Cherokees in adopting the
white man's "civilization" would make it "mortifying to common sense,
that their removal should be so repeatedly urged."

The Cherokee experiment with centralized government was only one more
facet of the many extraordinary changes that had taken place in native
customs, manners, and living conditions. A comparison of the provisions of
the Constitution of 1827 relating to blacks with the previous treatment of these
people by the Cherokees demonstrates one such change. Negro slavery had

increased noticeably among the Cherokees during the late eighteenth and early nineteenth centuries, primarily as a result of their renewed interest in agriculture following the continuing loss of tribal hunting lands and as a result of the example set by surrounding white plantations. A few full-scale Indian plantations based on slave labor were in existence in 1800. Many of the native slaveowners had long treated their slaves humanely; Indians and black slaves sometimes worked side by side and occasionally intermarried. Initially, there was comparatively little racial stigma or prejudice against blacks, but this benign treatment underwent a transformation during the 1820s.

By that time there were nearly 1,300 black slaves in the Cherokee Nation, and some Indians were anxious to purchase more to produce an agricultural surplus; to provide skilled labor for commercial, transportation, and manufacturing enterprises; and to increase their stature. The native elite, like their white neighbors, associated the ownership of blacks with social prominence, and the wealthier Cherokees used some slaves as servants in their homes or in their public buildings and taverns.

Again following the lead of white southerners, Indian slaveowners took steps to restrict the rights of the blacks they acquired. In some cases, the Cherokees even went further in this direction than did white slaveholding Tennesseans. In 1824 the Cherokee Nation forbade its citizens to intermarry with Negroes and prohibited black slaves from owning horses, cattle, or hogs. Three years later, at a time when free blacks were still eligible to vote in Tennessee, the Cherokee Constitution specifically withheld the right to vote from ''negroes and descendants of white and Indian men by negro women who may have been set free.'' The document also stipulated that ''no person who is of negro or mulatto parentage, either by the father or mother side, shall be eligible to hold any office of profit, honor or trust under this Government.'' The Cherokees had observed the treatment of blacks in neighboring white communities in Tennessee, Georgia, North Carolina, and Alabama; according to some tribal leaders, the debasement of the Negroes in their society would raise the Indians in the eyes of the whites.

Eight years after the adoption of the Cherokee Constitution, a little over 200 of the more than 16,500 Cherokees living in the South owned a total of nearly 1,600 slaves, including 480 blacks who lived in Tennessee. There were relatively few Cherokee-blacks or so-called ''mixed Negroes'' anywhere in the Cherokee Nation because of the proscription against intermarriage with blacks. Nevertheless, despite increasing restrictions on the blacks, the enduring power of Cherokee cultural traditions apparently ameliorated the harsher aspects of the slave codes that the Indian planters emulated. At least the absence of advertisements for runaway Indian slaves in the *Cherokee Phoenix* and the lack of Cherokee statutes dealing with insubordination by slaves stand out in stark contrast to the multitude of such notices and laws in the newspapers and statute books of neighboring white communities. The Cherokees, moreover, did not prohibit slaves from learning to read and write. Indeed, some slave children attended mission schools with Indian youths, and blacks continued to influence Cherokee acceptance of American culture—the white man's language, religion, farming techniques, and animal husbandry practices. Yet the trend toward the debasement of slaves continued.

The status of native women also changed as the Cherokees progressively adopted American cultural patterns. The high station that their political and social life had traditionally assigned women came under growing attack. In interacting with the Cherokees, Americans treated the men as the heads of their households and assumed that Indian families carried the name of their fathers. The increasingly large mixed blood population followed this practice, and soon the old pattern of descent through the mother broke down. The clan system was gradually replaced by the American pattern of husband-dominated households. By the time the last Beloved Woman of the Cherokees, Nancy Ward, died in 1822, the status of women in Cherokee society had fallen considerably, and five years later this decline was officially recognized in the Cherokee Constitution. Indian women were excluded from participation in the government and prohibited from voting. By limiting the rights of women, the natives had moved one more step along "the white man's road," for American men generally viewed domesticity and submissiveness as the proper roles for women to play in their society.

Regardless of the level of acceptance of white cultural patterns demonstrated by the Cherokee Constitution of 1827, the document brought about an immediate crisis in Indian-white relations in the South. Georgians reacted promptly to this example of Cherokee nationalism by passing legislation extending the state's legal jurisdiction over the Indians and by including in their county boundaries all Cherokee territory within their state. The white residents of Tennessee, North Carolina, and Alabama paid close attention to these moves.

Meanwhile, Andrew Jackson, the Tennessean who championed the relocation of all eastern Indians to a trans-Mississippi location, entered the White House in March 1829. Although Jackson had once encouraged missionary activity among the Cherokees to promote their acceptance of white "civilization," he had consistently maintained that the existence of Indian tribes within the sovereign states was not in the best interests of state or national development. To promote Indian emigration to the West, Jackson's supporters in Congress pushed through the Removal Bill of 1830, despite the opposition of fellow Tennessean David Crockett and numerous other politicians whose consciences or political inclinations caused them to vote against the measure.

The new legislation empowered Old Hickory to exchange public domain in the West for Indian land in the East if the Indians agreed to such a trade. Following the passage of the act, Secretary of War John Eaton offered to meet representatives of several southern tribes at the Masonic Hall in Franklin, Tennessee, to discuss the question of removal to the West. Only the Chickasaws sent tribal leaders to the parley. The Cherokees' refusal to attend the meeting marked the beginning of an eight-year struggle to defend their right to remain on their tribal domain.

Cherokee nationalism had deepened over the years with their accommodation to the ways of the Americans surrounding them. The development of the Cherokee syllabary, the establishment of a representative government, the appearance of a tribal newspaper, and the necessity of congregating together on an ever diminishing tribal domain helped the natives to overcome the regionalism and the disunity that had plagued them in earlier times. All of these factors contributed to the formulation, diffusion, and perpetuation of a group consciousness which solidified Cherokee national sentiment in the early 1830s. Under the able leadership of John Ross, these Indians decided not to cede another inch of their land to the United States and not to recognize the right of American states to legislate over them.

The Cherokee Nation looked to the Supreme Court of the United States as its savior. Encouraged by anti-Jacksonian politicians like Henry Clay, David Crockett, and Daniel Webster, the Cherokees hired former Attorney General William Wirt to protest the extension of the state laws of Georgia over them. On March 18, 1831, Chief Justice John Marshall delivered an ingenious opinion in the case of the *Cherokee Nation versus the State of Georgia*. Marshall accepted neither Wirt's contention that the Cherokees constituted a sovereign nation nor the Jackson administration's position that they were a subject nation completely at the mercy of Georgia. Marshall contended that Indian tribes were neither independent nor subject nations but "domestic dependent nations." According to the chief justice, the natives were "in a state of pupilage" and were "wards" of the federal government. While Marshall admitted that the American "guardian" was responsible for the

Two leaders of the Treaty party: John Ridge (*above*) and Major Ridge (*below*). From lithographs published by McKenney and Hall in *The Indian Tribes of North America, 1836–44*, and subsequent editions; courtesy of National Anthropological Archives, Smithsonian Institution.

welfare of its Indian wards, he nevertheless rejected the Cherokee Nation's petition for a restraining order to stop Georgia from interfering with its rights on the grounds that the tribe had incorrectly filed suit as a foreign nation.

Following Marshall's decision, life became hectic for the Cherokees as Georgia officials stepped up their campaign of intimidation and even arrested the Christian missionaries residing among them. A delegation of Cherokee leaders toured northeastern cities seeking funds to aid their people and encouraged Americans to petition Congress to support the tribe against the oppression of Georgia and to demand the release of the imprisoned missionaries. William Wirt brought the subject of the detention of the missionaries before the Supreme Court in the case of *Worcester versus the State of Georgia*. On March 3, 1832, Chief Justice Marshall ruled that Georgia's extension of state law over the Cherokees was unconstitutional and that the missionaries had to be released from jail. Technicalities in the federal laws relating to the enforcement of Supreme Court decrees, however, left the Cherokees at the mercy of Georgia.

As the harangues of Georgia state officials continued and as President Jackson relentlessly pressured the Indians to leave the South, two rival parties emerged in Cherokee politics. The majority National party was led by John Ross, who steadfastly refused to relinquish any of the remaining Cherokee lands to the United States. Opposed to Ross was the minority Treaty party led by Major Ridge, his ambitious son, John Ridge, and Major Ridge's nephew, Elias Boudinot. The Ridges and Boudinot had long fought to defend the Cherokee domain, but they now concluded that removal was inevitable. They argued that it was wiser to take the best terms possible from President Jackson rather than wait and incur the wrath of federal and state officials.

Between 1832 and 1835 Georgia officials secretly courted the Treaty party leaders and openly harassed supporters of the National party. In late 1832 the state prepared to force the Cherokees off their domain by distributing all Cherokee land to the winners of a lottery. As the lottery progressed, a horde of white invaders descended on the Cherokee country, acting with virtual impugnity since Georgia did not allow Indians to testify against whites in court. Whereas the Ridges and Elias Boudinot received assurances from Georgia Governor Wilson Lumpkin of protection against the intruders, the followers of John Ross were increasingly dispossessed of their property. When Ross himself returned to his beautiful mansion in Georgia from one of his innumerable and frustrating trips to Washington, he found a stranger living in his house. The irate principal chief of the Cherokee Nation, after locating his family, moved into a small, rough-hewed log cabin across the state line near the Red Clay council ground in present-day Bradley County, Tennessee.

Many supporters of the National party sought refuge in Tennessee because this state was not pushing its campaign to evict the Cherokees from its boundaries as aggressively as was Georgia. The Tennessee General Assembly passed an act in 1833 placing under its legal jurisdiction all Cherokee land within its borders, but the law protected Indian property rights and limited the criminal jurisdiction of the state courts in Cherokee country to cases involving larceny, murder, and rape. When an Indian named James Foreman contested this legislation, the state supreme court upheld its constitutionality. Chief Justice John Catron, in delivering his opinion in this case in 1835, remarked that "the truth is, neither our theory or practice has ever allowed to the Indians, any political right extending beyond our pleasure." Foreman, who eventually emigrated west, considered appealing this decision to the United States Supreme Court, but time was running out for the Indians.

The emergence of two rival factions in Cherokee politics had greatly complicated the Indian nation's domestic affairs, and the resulting strife enabled the United States War Department to secure its goal of relocating the Cherokees. The department worked through the Treaty party, just as did Georgia, which continued its harassment of the Indians who opposed the treaty. In the summer of 1835, for example, the Georgia Guard confiscated the press, other equipment, and supplies of the *Cherokee Phoenix* only hours before wagons sent by Ross arrived to remove these things to Tennessee. So aggressive was Georgia in its eviction campaign that shortly after the Indians rejected a proposed treaty in October 1835 at the Red Clay council ground an overzealous detachment of the Georgia Guard crossed into Tennessee and arrested Ross and the poet and playwright John Howard Payne who was visiting him. The guard detained Ross and Payne for over a week in Spring Place, Georgia. Although a storm of anger against Georgia arose in Tennessee after the *Knoxville Register* reported the invasion of Tennessee soil, the residency of Ross and other Cherokees in Tennessee was destined to be short.

On December 29, 1835, the leaders of the Treaty party and representatives of the United States, including former Tennessee Governor William Carroll, signed a removal treaty at New Echota, the Cherokee capital in Georgia. The overwhelming majority of the Indian nation claimed no association with the document, but the United States Senate ratified it by the extremely narrow margin of one vote. President Jackson proclaimed in May 1836 that the treaty was binding on all Cherokees and that they would have to emigrate from the South to the trans-Mississippi West within two years. Under the provisions of this "fraudulent treaty," as the National party referred to it, the United States Army soon began rounding up the Indians to prepare them for removal by the 1838 deadline.

The events surrounding the relocation of the Cherokees from Tennessee, Georgia, North Carolina, and Alabama to the West made it a virtual "Trail of

Tears," a far different journey from the one the Cherokees originally planned when they deliberately embarked on "the white man's road" years earlier.

In order to prepare the Cherokees for their removal to the West, the War Department dispatched army units to the Indian country. East Tennessee volunteers under Brigadier General Richard G. Dunlap also moved into action to prevent the National party from staging an uprising against the treaty. Between 1836 and May 23, 1838—the ultimate date set for the completion of voluntary removal—approximately 2,000 Cherokees journeyed west under the terms of the treaty. Some of these emigrants traveled in flatboats along the Tennessee, Ohio, Mississippi, and Arkansas rivers. Others took the overland route from the site of the old Cherokee Agency in Bradley County opposite Calhoun through McMinnville, Murfreesboro, Nashville, and Port Royal in Tennessee and then through Kentucky, Illinois, Missouri, and Arkansas. The leaders of the overland party which left Bradley County in October 1837 visited Andrew Jackson at the Hermitage as they passed through the Nashville area. Along the way to the West, these emigrants, even the wealthy mixed bloods, suffered from cholera, pellagra, and other diseases as well as from the hardships of the journey itself.

Meanwhile, the overwhelming majority of the Cherokees followed John Ross's leadership and refused to recognize the legitimacy of the treaty. As it became clear that they would not emigrate voluntarily, the War Department prepared for their forcible removal. General Dunlap was so impressed with the support for Ross that he disbanded his regiment in September 1836 and told his men that he would never dishonor Tennessee by "aiding to carry into execution at the point of the bayonet a treaty made by a lean minority against the will and authority of the Cherokee people."

Other soldiers rounded up the Cherokees at bayonet point and herded them into temporary, wooden stockades in preparation for their eviction. In the spring of 1838, President Martin Van Buren sent General Winfield Scott to the Cherokee Nation to direct the removal operations. Although Scott ordered his soldiers to treat the natives in a humane fashion, Baptist minister Evan Jones reported from a camp near Cleveland, Tennessee, that "the Cherokees are nearly all prisoners. They have been dragged from their houses and encamped at the forts and military posts, all over the nation." Forced without a moment's notice to abandon their homes, crops, and livestock, the Cherokees found themselves without sufficient clothing, bedding, cooking utensils, or other necessary possessions. General Scott admitted that the natives had suffered a tremendous "loss of their property consequent upon the hurry of capture and removal," but he charged that their misguided faith in the ability of Chief Ross to save them was the real source of their misfortune.

Life in the stockades for the Indians awaiting transportation west was very difficult. White contractors out to make a profit from the removal process frequently supplied them with spoiled food; medical care was also inadequate. Once the army had gathered some 15,000 Cherokees into the stockades, soldiers began taking parties to Ross's Landing and Calhoun in Tennessee and Gunter's Landing in Alabama for transportation by water to the West.

The mortality rate of the first 3,000 captive Indians who departed under military supervision was horribly high due to disease, exposure, fatigue, and other hardships of travel. By now John Ross and other leaders of the National party realized that the situation was hopeless. Thus Ross urged General Scott, who was sympathetic to the Cherokees' tragic situation, to allow the natives to supervise their own removal. From the Hermitage at Nashville, former President Jackson warned the Van Buren administration that it was "madness and folly" to allow the Cherokees to undertake such operations. Jackson feared that they would not stress "principles of economy." In spite of his warning, Van Buren followed Scott's advice and permitted the Indians to supervise their own removal.

On October 1, 1838, the first contingent emigrating under the supervision of Chief Ross began their westward trek, after the Cherokee Nation held a final council at Rattlesnake Springs near today's Charleston, Tennessee, where, by unanimous consent, the Indians agreed to continue to abide by their constitution and laws in the West. The group traveled overland, crossed the Tennessee River near the mouth of the Hiwassee River, moved northwest through McMinnville and Nashville, proceeded through Hopkinsville, Kentucky, and southern Illinois to Cape Girardeau, Missouri, and finally marched through southeastern Missouri and northern Arkansas to present-day Oklahoma. Later emigrant parties had to go through southwestern Missouri by way of Jackson, Springfield, and Southwest City because game along the first route had been depleted.

Not unlike the problems encountered by earlier groups, the conditions experienced en route by these emigrants were brutal: the journey was fatiguing, disease was rampant, and many greedy whites sought to cheat the Indians as they moved through frontier communities. Among the many who died on the way to the West was the wife of Chief John Ross. According to one traveler who observed their westward trek, the faces of the Cherokees carried "a downcast dejected look bordering upon the appearance of despair." By March 1839 the sad journey was over. The *Nunna-da-ult-sun-yi* ("the trail where they cried") had taken a tremendous toll among these Indians. Approximately 4,000 of the more than 17,000 Cherokees and their slaves who left the South under the treaty of 1835 died as a result of the trip or the circumstances surrounding their capture and detention before the emigration began. The

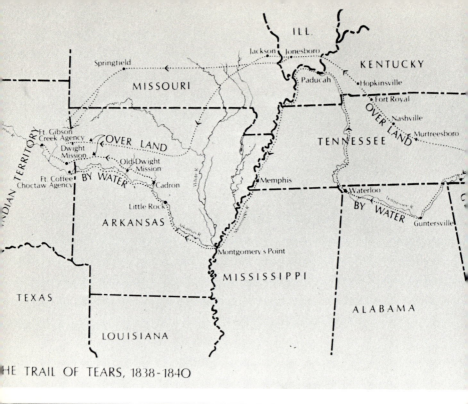

THE TRAIL OF TEARS, 1838-1840

Indians who went west after Ross had convinced the army to allow him to handle the emigration suffered a lower mortality rate than their kinsmen who had left earlier.

By late March 1839 the former Cherokee residents of Tennessee and neighboring southern states had completed their exodus from the South. Three months after the final group of emigrants arrived in the West, disgruntled antitreaty Cherokees sought revenge for the unauthorized sale of their ancient tribal homeland. Invoking the Blood Law of 1829, they brutally assassinated the Treaty party leaders—Major Ridge, his son John, and his nephew Elias Boudinot. Although the followers of John Ross outnumbered the remainder of the tribe, the Cherokees West or Old Settlers with whom the Treaty party had quickly merged were unwilling to yield control of their government to the new arrivals. Fortunately, spokesmen for moderation among the Old Settlers, such as Sequoyah, and among the Ross party, such as Reverend Jesse Bushyhead, were able to prevent the outbreak of civil war between the two groups. Under the influence of these men, leaders of the rival factions signed an Act of Union on July 12, 1839. John Ross then took the reins of leadership as the Cherokee Nation began a new phase in its history.

Not all of the Cherokees made the journey along the Trail of Tears, and not all who went to the West remained there. Some escaped from the soldiers and hid in the Great Smoky Mountains, where they were eventually joined by others who returned from the West. Tsali, a middle-aged Indian who lived on the Nantahala River in North Carolina, was one of those who escaped. According to the legend recorded by ethnologist James Mooney, Tsali argued with the soldiers taking him to the stockade at Calhoun, Tennessee, when one of them prodded his wife with a bayonet for walking too slowly. In a scuffle following this incident, Tsali or someone else killed a soldier, and Tsali and his family fled. Eventually, the United States made a bargain with Tsali. In return for his life and the lives of others in his family who were involved in the incident, the army agreed to allow the rest of the Cherokee fugitives to remain in the mountains until the government had time to settle their case.

Upon hearing this offer, so the story goes, Tsali, his brother, and his three sons gave themselves up. To impress the remaining fugitives with their helplessness against the American government, the army required Indian warriors to act as the firing squad. Tsali's youngest son was spared, however,

---

(*Above*): The Trail of Tears, 1838–40. From Earl Boyd Pierce and Rennard Strickland, *The Cherokee People*, by permission of the authors. (*Below*): "Trail of Tears" by Robert Lindneux. From the Original Oil Painting at Woolaroc Museum, Bartlesville, Oklahoma.

and after his father, uncle, and two brothers were buried in unmarked graves, he returned to the refugees in the mountains. Although scholars have challenged various details of the Tsali legend, there is general agreement that Tsali refused to abandon his homeland and that he eventually became a hero to the descendants of the Cherokee people who escaped removal to the West. Approximately 1,000 Cherokees, nearly all full bloods, remained in the dense wilderness of the Great Smoky Mountains by 1840. This small remnant was all that remained of the largest, most "civilized" Indian nation that ever lived in Tennessee.

Acknowledgments and Suggestions for Further Readings

During the course of my research, I have benefited from the assistance of a large number of people and institutions. It is a pleasure to acknowledge their contributions. Staff members at the Thomas Gilcrease Institute of American History and Art in Tulsa, the Joint University Libraries in Nashville, the Library of Congress, the Memphis State University Library, the Mississippi Department of Archives and History, the National Archives and Records Service, the Newberry Library in Chicago, the Oklahoma Historical Society, the Tennessee State Library and Archives, and the libraries of the University of Tennessee at Knoxville and Martin greatly facilitated my research. Part of the research incorporated into this study was supported by a grant from the Ford Foundation Ethnic Studies Program.

I am especially indebted to the following individuals for helping to improve the manuscript: Paul Bergeron and Charles H. Faulkner of the University of Tennessee at Knoxville, Brian M. Butler of the Tennessee Department of Conservation, Charles Hudson of the University of Georgia and his wife Joyce Rockwood Hudson, and Duane H. King of the Museum of the Cherokee Indian in Cherokee, North Carolina. My colleagues Ernest Blythe, Marvin Downing, John Eisterhold, Harry Hutson, Choong Soon Kim, Milton Simmons, Jimmy Trentham, Langdon Unger, and John Wittenberg also provided valuable assistance and encouragement. Jeanne King and Linda Davis painstakingly typed the various drafts of this manuscript. I am sincerely grateful to all of those named above for their contributions. Finally, I wish to express my deepest thanks and appreciation to the three very special people to whom this book is dedicated.

Further information about Tennessee's Indian peoples can be found in the books listed below:

GENERAL SURVEYS

Hudson, Charles. *The Southeastern Indians*. Knoxville: Univ. of Tennessee Press, 1976.

Lewis, Thomas M. N., and Madeline Kneberg. *Tribes That Slumber: Indians of the Tennessee Region*. Knoxville: Univ. of Tennessee Press, 1958.

EARLY ACCOUNTS

Adair, James. *The History of the American Indians*. 1775; rpt. ed., with an introduction by Samuel C. Williams. Johnson City, Tenn.: Watauga Press, 1930.

Haywood, John. *The Natural and Aboriginal History of Tennessee, up to the First Settlements Therein by the White People in the Year 1768*. 1823; rpt. ed., with an introduction by Mary U. Rothrock. Kingsport, Tenn.: F. M. Hill-Books, 1973.

Williams, Samuel Cole. *Early Travels in the Tennessee Country 1540–1800*. Johnson City, Tenn.: Watauga Press, 1928.

THE CHICKASAW, CREEK, AND SHAWNEE INDIANS

Alford, Thomas Wildcat. *Civilization: As Told to Florence Drake*. Norman: Univ. of Oklahoma Press, 1936.

Baird, W. David. *The Chickasaw People*. Phoenix: Indian Tribal Series, 1974.

Clark, Jerry E. *The Shawnee*. Lexington: Univ. Press of Kentucky, 1977.

Corkran, David H. *The Creek Frontier 1540–1783*. Norman: Univ. of Oklahoma Press, 1967.

Debo, Angie. *The Road to Disappearance*. Norman: Univ. of Oklahoma Press, 1941.

Eggleston, George Cary. *Red Eagle and the Wars with the Creek Indians of Alabama*. New York: Dodd, Mead, 1878.

Gibson, Arrell M. *The Chickasaws*. Norman: Univ. of Oklahoma Press, 1971

Green, Donald E. *The Creek People*. Phoenix: Indian Tribal Series, 1973.

Malone, James H. *The Chickasaw Nation: A Short Sketch of a Noble People*. Louisville: John P. Morton, 1922.

Swanton, John R. *Early History of the Creek Indians and Their Neighbors*. Washington, D. C.: Government Printing Office, 1922.

Tucker, Glenn. *Tecumseh: Vision of Glory*. Indianapolis: Bobbs-Merrill, 1956.

THE CHEROKEES

Brown, John P. *Old Frontiers: The Story of the Cherokee Indians from Earliest Times to the Date of Their Removal to the West, 1838*. 1938; rpt. New York: Arno Press & *New York Times*, 1971.

Corkran, David H. *The Cherokee Frontier: Conflict and Survival, 1740–1762.* Norman: Univ. of Oklahoma Press, 1962.

Forman, Grant. *Sequoyah.* Norman: Univ. of Oklahoma Press, 1938.

Gabriel, Ralph Henry. *Elias Boudinot, Cherokee and His America.* Norman: Univ. of Oklahoma Press, 1941.

Gearing, Fred. *Priests and Warriors: Social Structures for Cherokee Politics in the 18th Century.* Menasha, Wis.: American Anthropological Assoc., 1962.

Kilpatrick Jack Frederick. *Sequoyah of Earth & Intellect.* Austin: Encino Press, 1965.

Malone, Henry T. *Cherokees of the Old South: A People in Transition.* Athens: Univ. of Georgia Press, 1956.

Mooney, James. *Myths of the Cherokee and Sacred Formulas of the Cherokees.* 1900; rpt., Nashville: Charles Elder, 1972.

Moulton, Gary E. *John Ross: Cherokee Chief.* Athens: Univ. of Georgia Press, 1978.

Perdue, Theda. *Slavery and the Evolution of Cherokee Society, 1540–1866.* Knoxville: Univ. of Tennessee Press, 1979.

Pierce, Earl Boyd and Rennard Strickland. *The Cherokee People.* Phoenix: Indian Tribal Series, 1973.

Reid, John Phillip. *A Law of Blood: The Primitive Law of the Cherokee Nation.* New York: New York Univ. Press, 1970.

Starkey, Marion L. *The Cherokee Nation.* New York: Knopf, 1946.

Wilkins, Thurman. *Cherokee Tragedy: The Story of the Ridge Family and of the Decimation of a People.* New York: Macmillan, 1970.

Woodward, Grace Steele. *The Cherokees.* Norman: Univ. of Oklahoma Press, 1963.

INDIAN-WHITE RELATIONS

Cotterill, R. S. *The Southern Indians: The Story of the Civilized Tribes Before Removal.* Norman: Univ. of Oklahoma Press, 1954.

Foreman, Grant. *Indian Removal: The Emigration of the Five Civilized Tribes of Indians.* New ed., Norman: Univ. of Oklahoma Press, 1953.

Horsman, Reginald. *Expansion and American Indian Policy, 1783–1812.* East Lansing: Michigan State Univ. Press, 1967.

O'Donnell, James H., III. *Southern Indians in the American Revolution.* Knoxville: Univ. of Tennessee Press, 1973.

Prucha, Francis Paul. *American Indian Policy in the Formative Years: The Indian Trade and Intercourse Acts, 1790–1834.* Cambridge, Mass.: Harvard Univ. Press, 1962.

Remini, Robert V. *Andrew Jackson and the Course of American Empire, 1767–1821*. New York: Harper & Row, 1977.

Satz, Ronald N. *American Indian Policy in the Jacksonian Era*. Lincoln: Univ. Of Nebraska Press, 1975.

Van Every, Dale. *Disinherited: The Lost Birthright of the American Indian*. New York: Morrow, 1966.

Index

(References to illustrations are in **bold type**)

Other Tennessee Three Star Books

Visions of Utopia
Nashoba, Rugby, Ruskin, and the ''New Communities'' in Tennessee's Past
by John Egerton

Our Restless Earth
The Geologic Regions of Tennessee
by Edward T. Luther

Tennessee Strings
The Story of Country Music in Tennessee
by Charles K. Wolfe

Paths of the Past
Tennessee, 1770–1970
by Paul H. Bergeron

Civil War Tennessee
Battles and Leaders
by Thomas L. Connelly